Awake to Life Aware of God

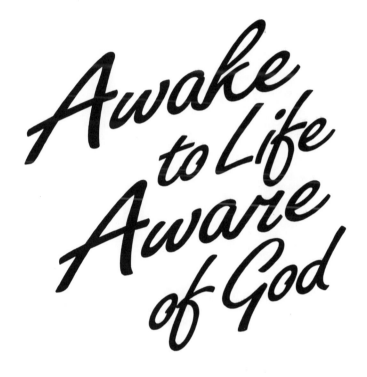

Awake to Life Aware of God

Kenneth E. Grabner, C.S.C.

AVE MARIA PRESS Notre Dame, Indiana 46556

© 1994 by Ave Maria Press, Inc., Notre Dame, IN 46556

International Standard Book Number: 0-87793-530-0

Library of Congress Catalog Card Number: 94-70328

Cover and text design by Elizabeth J. French

Photography:
Robert Campbell 130; Vernon Sigl 6, 14, 50, 94; Bob Taylor cover, 164.

Printed and bound in the United States of America.

Contents

Introduction ✧ 7

ONE

Noticing What's Here ✧ 15

TWO

Gateways to a Fully Conscious Life ✧ 51

THREE

The Obstacles to a Fully Conscious Life ✧ 95

FOUR

Alive Throughout the Ages to Come ✧ 131

Epilogue ✧ 165

Introduction

"I feel so scattered and distracted," the young woman said to the teacher. "What can I do to get my life in shape?"

"If you want to come alive," the teacher answered, "be awake to what is happening in the present moment. Be fully aware of each moment as it is given to you. But once you set your feet on the path of awareness, be careful not to turn away from it. Otherwise you will sleep through the adventure of life."

Jesus said, "Anyone who starts to plow and then keeps looking back is of no use for the Kingdom of God."

—Luke 9:62

"Are you awake to life?" It is a worthwhile question to ask yourself. In fact, the whole task of life is to be awake to your life experiences, to be fully conscious of the present moment. Otherwise, you are not as alive as you could be. Your consciousness is not where your body is.

Being fully conscious means being awake to your physical sensations as you experience them in your daily life. If you happen to be walking, being fully conscious means being aware of your bodily sensations as you walk. That may sound mundane, but the next time you are out for a walk, pay attention to what it feels like. Many people never know, because their minds are not with them as they walk. They are either planning for the future or mulling over the past.

Being fully conscious means being dynamically aware of your environment, awake to what is happening around you in your present moment. Fully conscious people notice their surroundings. They notice the beauties of nature and they appreciate God's handiwork. When they are in contact with other people, they are fully attentive to them. Their attentiveness enables them to appreciate others and to respond to them as individuals with their own unique personalities and needs. Fully conscious people are open to the goodness of life, and at the same time, are able to learn from the sufferings that are an inseparable part of life.

Being fully conscious means being peacefully aware that God is not a stranger to you or your world. Fully conscious people perceive the intimate, compassionate presence of God within themselves and within the entirety of creation. In the realization of this presence, they discover that they are

nourished, sustained, and loved. It is in this awareness
that they discover the deepest meaning of life.

*Being fully conscious means savoring the joy and wholeness
that flow from your inner life experiences and from your awareness of the world around you.* We are fulfilled only by becoming conscious—conscious of God's loving presence in and
around us, conscious of ourselves, conscious of the world
that flows from God's hands. Over time, we begin to find
that our consciousness is like a multi-colored rainbow. We
discover that it embraces many beautiful and different
experiences that make up the fullness our lives are meant
to be. The more alive we are, the more we become aware
of the various facets of consciousness that give our lives
meaning. And yet, we know from our own experience that
living a truly conscious life is difficult. How many of us
are truly awake to the experiences of our lives? How many
of us are fully aware of our surroundings, of others, of
ourselves, of the God who permeates all of creation.

*Being fully conscious means experiencing communion with
God, with your brothers and sisters, with yourself, with everything that is.* It is this experience of communion that brings
us a sense of wholeness and belonging. Through our
loving response to reality, we discover our union with it.
This is a joy open to all people who are willing to grow in
their ability to become ever more conscious and awake
through the giving and receiving of love.

This book is about the many experiences of consciousness that make up life and our need to become awake to
them. The aim is not to stratify them or put them in some
kind of hierarchical order. Our stream of consciousness is
usually too fluid and uncontainable for such pigeon-
holing. Yet, in order to reflect on the experience of consciousness we have to break the experience down into

digestible concepts. The important thing to realize, though, is that concepts are just concepts. They can only become meaningful if they are experienced. If we become lovingly and compassionately awake in our lives, we finally become aware of everything.

This book begins with a series of reflections on what we are able to experience when we become more awake, and what happens to us when we pay more attention to our present moment. Growth into deeper consciousness is a life-long journey that can only be successfully undertaken with patience and faith. Being fully awake is not the normal state for most of us. We have to work at achieving a deeper state of wakefulness, and this is more difficult than it might seem.

One of the keys to becoming more awake is to develop a state of mind that leads to a loving consciousness. When we do this we discover that there are many "gateways to consciousness." These gateways are the attitudes and activities that help us to become more aware of our lives and our relationships. Another key to becoming more awake is to recognize the obstacles that hinder us in our growth toward a loving consciousness and to attempt to root them out. Our obstacles are the negative attitudes and actions that have the power to sabotage our growth toward deeper consciousness. Our attitudes and lifestyles are either our enemies or our allies. The two midsections of this book deal with these topics.

Our journey toward consciousness is not for this life only. Through death, the journey is transformed and it continues on another plane. Those with a dynamic belief in the resurrection may sometimes wonder what this experience will be like. It is not an idle consideration. The resurrected life is our ultimate goal. In the resurrected life, we experience the fullness of what we are meant to be.

While much of the meaning of the resurrected life is

shrouded in mystery, we can know something about it through scripture. We can also understand something about it by making analogies to certain experiences that we have in this life. Understanding what we can of the resurrected life helps us to put this life in a better focus. The last section of this book deals with these topics.

Each of the four major sections is divided into short topical reflections. Although one topic flows into the next, each one is a complete unit in itself. This arrangement makes it possible to read this book a few minutes at a time without losing continuity. The prayer and suggestions for experiential exercises that follow each topic offer the opportunity to assimilate it into your own personal experience. You might also decide to keep a journal in which you write down your thoughts. This practice will help you to read this book not only with your mind, but also with your heart. Only by reading with the heart can you go beyond the concepts to the experiences which underlie them and come to full understanding.

When we try to speak about conscious awareness, about waking up to a deeper unity with God and with all of God's creation, there is always a problem with words. Imagine trying to describe the color green, or the sweet taste of an orange. Words can never adequately convey the actual experience of colors and tastes. Words express concepts, but concepts are poor substitutes for actual experience. If we stop with the words, we miss the point. Words are meant to lead to an awareness beyond what language can express. As you read this book, let the words lead you to your own experiences. If you think about the words and go beyond them, then the words may have value for you. Otherwise, the words remain just words.

When speaking about God we face an additional problem with words. Because it is almost impossible to speak of God without using personal pronouns, we sometimes wind up assigning a gender to God. When, for the sake of grammatical convention, masculine pronouns are used, no bias is intended. God knows who God is no matter what we call him or her. And, gender-wise at least, we know who we are, too!

All of us are on a journey in which we grow not only in age, but ideally, also in wisdom, love, and compassion. Each one of us makes this journey alone, in the sense that we are the only ones who can make our own choices and know our own experiences. And yet we can help one another on the journey by encouraging each other and by sharing our insights. It is in caring deeply about one another's journeys that we most clearly show ourselves to be brothers and sisters. We cannot care about the journeys of others, however, unless we are sufficiently awake to care deeply about our own.

The joy of the journey is experienced only by those who keep forging ahead without looking back. Looking back is useless. It is the present moment that counts. Those who live fully in the present moment are the ones who hear God's siren-like call, a call that leads them into an ever fuller future.

ONE

Noticing What's Here

A wise, elderly woman was admired for her peace and contentment. They seemed to come from her as naturally as rays come from the sun. A young man approached her and said, "My life is so full of anxieties while yours seems so filled with contentment. What is your secret?"

"Learn to pay attention to the beauty within you and around you," she said. "Then you'll have less energy for your anxieties. You'll have more energy to be aware of what is real in the present moment. You'll become more fully alive and then you'll be content."

Jesus said, "I have come in order that you might have life—life in all its fullness."

—John 10:10

No one can be fully alive without learning how to be awake.

Being awake? Well, aren't you already awake? To some extent, the answer would have to be yes. Your eyes see this page. Your ears hear the sounds around you. Maybe they can even "hear" the silence that punctuates the sounds. But it takes more than eyes to see what is real, and more than ears to hear life's sounds and notice its silence.

A bumper sticker flashed this message on a crowded Western freeway: "Having a wonderful time. Wish I were here." And, of course, that's the problem. If we're not where we are, our eyes and ears aren't enough to tell us that we're having a good time. In order to have a good time, we have to be fully alive in the place where we are. How can we tell if that's the case? We have to ask ourselves how often we notice anything that arouses joy and a sense of wonder within us. Without joy and wonder, everyone misses what life is always ready and waiting to give. Life's gifts are in front of us and within us. The question is whether or not we are where the gifts are.

The book of Genesis tells us that when God created us, he made us in his own image. We are made in the image of an infinite, loving consciousness. An infinite, loving consciousness—that's one way to define God. God is forever lovingly conscious of what he has made, fully awake to his creation. If God were able to be unaware of what he had made—if God were to forget his creation— then you and I, along with all God's handiwork, would simply disappear. It is in the image of this lovingly conscious God that we are made. The more awake we are, the more we are like the God who caused us to be. The more we resemble God, the more we share in God's joy.

What does it mean to be awake, to be lovingly conscious?

And if we are asleep, how do we become awake? And most of all, what difference does any of this make in our everyday life? We already have some idea of the answer. To be awake means to live in the present moment, noticing everything that the present moment brings us. Gently pulling our attention back to what is happening in our present moment, we become more attuned to the gifts in our lives that we might have previously missed. We become awake to the goodness of our own lives. What flows from this kind of consciousness is a sense of peace and wholeness that we are meant to experience in the midst of our everyday activities.

Jesus came that we might have life, life in all its fullness. God wants us to notice fully the life given us as a gift. If we miss the gift, we miss the giver. The more conscious we are, the more we experience the One who loves us, the One in whose image we are made.

You surround me with your loveliness, my God,
and you make your home deep within me,
but I often fail to notice you where you are.
Are you perhaps challenging me to stay awake?
Are you challenging me to become more conscious of
    your presence within myself and within everything you
    have made?
Help me to be where you are, my God,
for you are in the midst of my life.
That is where I would like to be,
totally aware of what is happening within and around me.
I thank you for the gift of life.
I count on you for the ability to live more deeply

that I might be more fully conscious
of the many ways in which you reveal yourself to me.

When you notice your mind wandering into the past or
the future, bring it back to the present moment and pay
attention to what you are seeing or hearing. Learn to be
where you are.

Look at something beautiful in nature that you usually
tend to ignore. Offer thanks to God for the gift of creation,
as well as for the gift of consciousness that enables you to
appreciate it.

Consciousness is like a smorgasbord of delights that God sets in front of us.

Imagine two people on a lake shore. One of the persons
notices the waves of the lake as they break on the shore.
She watches the birds as they circle for fish, and then she
walks along the shore, awake to some of the unusually-
shaped colored stones that she picks up and examines with
enjoyment. She breathes deeply to catch the smell of the
lake, and then closes her eyes, concentrating on the cool
breeze blowing through her hair.

Several hundred yards away is a woman with a calculator in her hand. She owns a long stretch of land along
the lake shore, and she's punching in figures to see how
much money she can make if she subdivides the property
and sells it.

Which of the two is more alive to the beauty of the lake
and its environment? It isn't that the calculating should be
eliminated, but that it needs to be complemented by
awareness. Suppose that the woman with the calculator
never experienced the joy of noticing the lake; or suppose

that her ability to notice it died with her childhood. Wouldn't something be missing from her appreciation of life?

Where are you in relation to this story? With what kind of consciousness do you live your life? What kind of consciousness do you want for yourself?

To a great extent, the way you experience your life in this present moment is the result of your choice. Although your environment and past experiences have an impact on what you direct your attention to in life, you are always free to modify the impact. Freedom begins when you become aware of the habitual way you look at your life. It develops when you become aware of the different ways in which you could look at your life. Perhaps Jesus meant something similar when he said, "For your heart will always be where your riches are" (Luke 12:34).

When it comes to the experience of conscious awareness, life offers a smorgasbord of choices. The story of the women on the beach is only one example of the choices before us, but it is an important one. To walk in nature with awareness is a choice to discover the creative love of God through the things God has made. By paying attention to what we see, we experience God's creation as a gift to us. We grow in awareness of God's beauty and power shining through all of God's creative activity. We encounter God personally. God the creator speaks to us through creation. And in the encounter, we realize that we are loved.

Awareness of nature's ever changing beauty is only one of the aspects of life that consciousness opens to us. The joy of human love is yet another. Do we take the love of our friends for granted, not appreciating the many expressions through which this love shows itself? Imagine being invited to a meal by a friend and not tasting the love with which it was prepared, or receiving a gift and being unaware of the care with which it was selected. Sometimes, all appearances to the contrary, we are not awake.

The choice to be conscious of others could extend even to those who are not our friends. Thus, we begin to become conscious of our oneness with all of our brothers and sisters. The Bible considers love of God and love of others to be indivisible. It tells us that we cannot have one without the other. Indivisibility of love begins as a response to faith, but it is an experience that often becomes more personal through the practice of meditation, prayer, and service to others.

The opportunities to grow in consciousness are as varied as life itself. When we pay greater attention to the work we do, walk when we walk, eat when we eat, and actually be where we are, the parade of sensations is endless. We simply experience the joy of being alive, of doing what we are doing. There is really not much to accomplishing this kind of consciousness. The key is simply to pay full attention to what we are doing in the present moment. It is through attentiveness that we discover what it means to be fully alive right now, in the place where we are.

Paradoxically, though, there is a problem with this kind of attention. Learning to live in the present and letting the future take care of itself sounds simple enough. But it is difficult. It is not that we will stop making plans for the future, but that we will spend less time making them. We'll stop thinking about the future so much that we forget to live in the present. The solution to this propensity for being somewhere else in time is quite simple: keep pulling yourself back to the present moment. Practice experiencing the present.

The present moment is all we have. Paying attention to

where we are is all there is to it. But the possibility of doing that seems to escape many of us. And yet the utter simplicity of just being where we are is positively embarrassing!

Being fully conscious also has something to do with the way we pay proper attention to ourselves. Many of us never learn from the mistakes we make in life, and so we are destined to repeat them. Others never discover the unconscious influences that affect them because they pay no attention to their dreams and never try to figure out the real meaning of their fantasies. Here we have the language of the unconscious, the unknown element that is a part of each one of us. We can discover these aspects of ourselves through meditation, or with a qualified counselor who can help us to discover their meaning. With the exception of God, no one is closer to us than ourselves. If we do not know ourselves, we live with a stranger.

As rich as all of the above examples of conscious experience are, they do not exhaust our possibilities. Consciousness of our inner life opens up a whole new vista. Quieting the mind and coming to the center of ourselves, we learn to experience God's presence within us. In this experience, we know that we are loved, and we are gifted with a deep sense of peace. This too belongs to the fullness of what we can experience. It is a foretaste of the resurrected life which is given even in this life. We prepare for this experience through the practice of meditation, a quieting of the mind which allows God to make his presence felt within us.

Without a longing for wider levels of awareness and greater depths of consciousness, we remain asleep. Although all forms of consciousness are God's gifts, we are unlikely to taste them if we have no desire for them. The first step is the desire to be more awake. But even that desire itself is God's gift to us.

Life is a feast of consciousness, my God,
and the feast is your gift to me.
May I not spurn your gift by preferring to remain asleep.
Help me to wake up.
May I learn to find life an adventure,
a journey into ever wider and deeper realms of
    consciousness.
May I be faithful in savoring the life that you have set
    before me,
and prepare myself to become more fully awake.

Recall the story of the two persons on the beach. Each sees reality in a different way. With which person can you most closely identify? Is there some way in which you might want to broaden your vision of life? Would you like to become more awake? How will you start?

Life reveals its mysteries only to those who are fully alive.

Is it true that only privileged people experience the joy of being fully conscious of life's gifts? Or is this experience meant for all of us? What about the poor, the powerless, those who suffer, and those who are unloved? Even if none of those circumstances applies to us, we might think that if our own life circumstances were more favorable, perhaps we might be more fully alive. But then, perhaps favorable life circumstances aren't really necessary for developing a joyful consciousness of life.

A man in a concentration camp once was asked how he had been able to survive for so many years in the brutal conditions of camp confinement. His answer? He looked at his questioner and said, "At night, I look at the vast numbers of stars in the sky. In winter, I look at the beauty of the snow. In summer, I appreciate the flowers. You see, some of them grow even in places like this. And then sometimes, I just look up at the sky and watch the birds. And you know, even the cloud formations say something of the beauty of God."

What a grand message! Even in the most brutal conditions of life, something beautiful can be found. More than likely, our living conditions are not so terrible as this man's were. Why is it that in the midst of all the blessings that surround us, we manage to notice so little? Are some people just naturally more awake than others? Most of us have to work at becoming conscious. Without the effort, many of life's gifts go unnoticed. If we have been selling ourselves short and sleepwalking through life, how can we manage to become more alive to the beauty that surrounds us?

We have to start by wanting to love life. We notice what we really love. How can we increase our love of life? Perhaps by noticing more deeply what surrounds us, and what is inside of us. The procedure is circular. If we want to love, we must start noticing life. The more we notice, the more our love is able to grow. And the more our love grows, the more we will notice the things we love. Perhaps the whole process starts with an act of faith that life is worth loving. If we want to believe that more deeply, we have to make a choice to live more intensely. We have to live more consciously in the present moment, noticing what's here in front of us. What we notice in each moment will tell us something about God and about ourselves.

One day a person noticed a flower blooming in the

midst of a patch of rubble. All around the flower were chunks of concrete, broken wine bottles, empty cans and weeds. Steel mill smoke swirled around the flower and coated its leaves with a gritty, gray layer of dust. And yet the flower survived, just like the inmate in the concentration camp who kept himself alive by noticing the birds and the stars. The flower's message? We can survive anywhere, if we really want to. But flowers like that only speak their messages to people awake enough to notice.

Being awake is not only a condition of joy, sometimes it is a condition of survival. The man in the concentration camp survived because he was awake to the things that could spark his life. Isn't it the same for us? How often do we become ill because we're asleep to the things that bring meaning to us? When we don't sense an adequate meaning in our lives, we jeopardize our health. Our minds and bodies influence each other. The joys and sorrows of one are the joys and sorrows of the other. Being awake to God's presence in God's gifts is a condition of our joy and our well-being that touches both our bodies and our minds.

Our level of well-being deepens according to the perception of meaning in our lives. The more we perceive the loving presence of God within ourselves, and the more we try to discover this presence in the world around us, the more life's meaning shows itself. But mere head knowledge will never be a proof of this. The experience must touch not only our heads, but also our hearts; not only our minds, but also our bodies.

How does this begin to happen? Perhaps by doing what the inmate of the concentration camp did. Be fully aware of what you see. Then, calm your mind, have faith in God's presence, and notice what is going on inside of you. Every part of you becomes more alive.

"So then, you also must always be ready, because the Son of Man will come at an hour when you are not expect-

ing him," Jesus said (Matthew 24:44). Be ready for what?
For that final moment when God calls us into eternity?
What about all the other moments in which God is present
to us? God comes to us each day in myriad little joys that
surround our lives. But if we're asleep, how shall we
recognize God when God comes?

Help me to stay awake, my God,
so that the best parts of my life won't pass unnoticed.
I'm sorry that I've missed so much.
Could it be true that the meaning of conversion
is to become aware of your love
in all of the ways in which it surrounds me?
But what if I miss it?
If I really want to love you,
I'll have to notice all of the ways
in which you reveal your love through your gifts.
But you know my tendency to fall asleep.
Just as you are always conscious of me,
help me to become more conscious of you,
to notice you in the people and things
that I tend to take for granted.

Where do you most experience the presence of God in
your daily life? Where do you least experience God's
presence? Make an effort to become more conscious in
those areas of your life where you tend to be asleep.

You can be awake and asleep at the same time.

Awake and asleep at the same time? That may seem impossible, but many of us accomplish this paradoxical feat as a matter of course.

In the popular *Calvin and Hobbes* comic strip, Calvin often sits staring at his teacher as she writes on the chalkboard or at his parents as they scold him for some minor disobedience. He seems awake, but his mind is flying throughout the universe, visiting distant planets, and duelling with space demons. Awake and asleep at the same time! Adult versions of this phenomenon take on all kinds of curious forms. We have a tendency to ignore what is happening in the present moment and to make mental journeys elsewhere. We all have our own ways of being asleep, of not being fully where we are.

Our ways of being conscious can take a number of different paths. It is possible to be awake to one path of consciousness and to be oblivious to the others. Jesus tells the parable of the great feast which is a symbol for the presence of God (cf. Luke 14:15-24). Attending the feast could be described as sharing a union of consciousness with the host. The invitation to the feast symbolizes our invitation to be one with God in a conscious union of love. Unfortunately, the people who are invited refuse to come. They lack the desire to be conscious of more than their own most immediate needs. One had to look at a recently purchased field, another felt the need to try out a new pair of oxen, and a third had just gotten married. These people were probably quite adept at meeting the needs of the moment. What they lacked was the desire for intimate conscious communion with their God. Where they should have been eagerly awake, they were asleep.

In Luke 16:8 the idea is put this way, "The people of this world are much more shrewd in handling their affairs than the people who belong to the light." The statement challenges us to ask ourselves in which areas of our lives we are awake, and in which areas we are asleep. We reach the ideal when we become awake in many areas of our lives: when we are attuned to God's presence, when our interest is aroused by all of the beauty in our lives, and when we can respond appropriately to the needs of others. It is in the midst of our daily lives lived consciously with faith and love that we become conscious of God whose presence permeates us.

In this sense, we would not have to choose between our conscious union with God and involvement with the activities of our daily lives. At any given moment, we could be conscious of both. There is a catch, though. Without frequent periods of quiet prayer, we lose our ability to be aware of God's presence in the midst of our daily activities. That is why, in the language of the parable, the host invites his guests to forget their fields and oxen for the moment and simply come to the feast. If we take no time to be with our God in silence and in quiet, we will never be aware of our God in the midst of noise and activity. It is in the silence and quiet that our minds are attuned to the God who is always there. Without some experience of silence, we simply drown in the pool of our own noise. Work can become prayer only when it comes from a heart and mind that are still.

We can be conscious on many levels and we can be asleep on many levels. How can we tell when we are conscious, and when we are asleep? It isn't easy. You can be working hard and still be asleep. You can be giving a talk and be asleep. What if you give a talk and what you say comes from your head and not your heart? Then probably neither you nor your audience will be fully awake.

There is an infallible way to tell if we are awake. We can

tell that by the kind of life we lead. Jesus told his hearers to be on guard against false prophets, and that these prophets could be identified by what they do (Matthew 7:15-16). We know trees by the fruit they bear. Analogously we know people by the fruit they bear. If we are honest, we know something of ourselves by the fruit we produce. If we are false to ourselves and not awake, the fruit we bear isn't appetizing. If we are true to ourselves and lovingly conscious, the fruit we bear is magnificent. The most delightful people are those who are fully alive. They radiate peace and calm even in the midst of life's difficulties. They are joyful and compassionate even in circumstances that are hard. In short, they are lovingly conscious, fully awake. Who are these people? They are the ones who inspire and sustain us by their generosity and love of life. Society cannot do without them, and they are easy to identify. By their fruits, we will know them.

You have invited me to the feast, my God,
and like the other invited guests, I have sometimes
     declined your invitation.
I have often chosen not to be awake to your presence.
You offer me the gift of full consciousness which is meant
     to be my full joy.
Unfortunately, I too have gone out "to see my fields and
     test my oxen."
Many times I never really cared much about your
     invitation,
and in those times, I lost the sense of who I was.
I apologize for that,
but you see, many times I acted out of ignorance.

I didn't really understand what I was refusing.
I know you understand that.
What I want to do now is to open my heart to
      your presence
not only in the quiet of my mind,
but also in the midst of my daily activities.
May I discover your presence not only in the depths of
      my heart,
but even in the seemingly insignificant events of my
      daily life.
May I discover you in the service I give and receive
      from others.
And as your life grows in me,
may the fruit I bear be of value for others.

Ask yourself if you miss a great amount of the beauty
of your life by smothering yourself with excessive activity.
What is it that God is inviting you to experience more
deeply in your life? What kinds of preoccupations keep
you from responding to the invitation?

Life's gifts appear to those who notice the pennies, nickels, and dimes.

A friend of mine was resting comfortably on a small
rubber raft in the Caribbean Sea when he noticed a fifty
dollar bill floating by. It bobbed up and down so close to
his raft that he merely had to reach out and pick it up. A
common occurrence? Well, not really, at least not for most
of us. But in the parking lots of America, pennies, nickels,
and dimes can be found by the dozens, ready for the
taking.

Smart people know that life offers plenty of pennies, nickels, and dimes, but rarely a fifty dollar bill. The major joy of being awake is being aware of the small joys that come into our lives. There is no other way to be fully present to our lives, because life consists mostly of small, commonplace things and events.

We miss many of the small joys because we take them for granted. They're so much a part of our lives that we fail to see them. Contentment with life depends on our being aware of the small joys, because they form the building blocks of our daily life experiences. How does the awareness of these building blocks grow?

Start with the love and the friendships that perhaps we may undervalue or take for granted. Our friendships may seem ordinary to us, much less than what they really are. How much do we appreciate and enjoy our friends? These are among God's greatest gifts to us, but even the most valuable and precious friendships lose their luster when mutual relationships become routine. Human relationships keep their freshness when we look at them from a fresh point of view, with a mind open to the realization that each relationship is a gift that constantly reveals something new. If we're awake, we discover that. The problem is that many of our relationships seem ordinary to us, and so we look for extraordinary ones which never seem to come. Perhaps, more than we realize, we've already been extraordinarily blessed in the relationships that we have in the present moment. Would a deeper awareness of the people close to us make that realization come alive?

The same could be true for many of the other gifts in our lives. Some years ago, the electric company ran an advertisement to show how different our lives would be if there were no electricity. The ad portrayed a home full of appliances: a television set with VCR, a radio, a refrigerator, many lamps, and a clock. Each of these items was crossed out with a big X. Without electricity, none of these items would be of any value. We take electricity for granted, but without it, our lives would change dramatically. The point? How much do we appreciate the value of the electricity that forms such an ordinary part of our life? Could you imagine your life without a daily hot shower? How would a deeper appreciation of all of this add to the enjoyment of your life?

A simple example—the next time you turn on the hot water faucet, notice what comes out. Be aware of the pleasure and convenience as you do such a simple thing as washing your hands. Of course, life is full of many such simple pleasures, but we get so used to them that we fail to notice and enjoy them. And we fail to be thankful. When we are on the lookout for the ordinary pleasures of life, we discover quite a few of them. We might notice what our body feels like when we walk, what the wind feels like as it touches our face, what the trees sound like when the wind sings through their leaves. Life offers many things like that to us, but what happens when we are asleep and fail to notice?

How do we take what seem to be the pennies, nickels, and dimes of this life and make them into something extraordinary? By paying attention, by becoming awake to their presence and the joy they give. For the awake person, there are no pennies, nickels, and dimes, because there is no longer anything ordinary. For one who is continuously awake, all things can become a source of fresh enjoyment. Is it really possible to look at life from this point of view? It is if we take a different perspective and become more awake to all the gifts that continually surround us and bring us joy.

How can we become awake and stay awake? If we want to learn to ride a bicycle there is no other way than to get on it and start pedalling. So it is with our appreciation of all those realities that we might regard as pennies, nickels, and dimes. We become aware of their value by opening our eyes and taking a good look. We have to look and pay attention, and slowly we may become aware of values that, perhaps for a long time, we haven't noticed. There is nothing complicated in this type of experience. Could personal benefits come from anything so simple? It seems too good to be true, but there is only way we will ever know. We have to try it out for ourselves.

Jesus told a story about a man who gave each of his servants a sum of money. While the man was gone, each servant was to make a profit from the money he had been given. When the man returned, he called in the servants and asked for an accounting.

> The first one came and said, "Sir, I have earned ten gold coins with the one you gave me." "Well done," he said: "you are a good servant! Since you were faithful in small matters, I will put you in charge of ten cities" (Luke 19:16-17).

The first servant did all right. He used what had been given to him. It was quite a different matter though, with the unsuccessful servant who did nothing with his coin. Do you remember what his master said about him?

> "Take the gold coin away from him and give it to the servant who has ten coins." But they said to him, "Sir, he already has ten coins!" "I tell you," he replied, "that to every person who has something, even more will be given; but the person who has nothing, even the little that he has will be taken away from him" (Luke 19:24-26).

The point? What we don't use is eventually lost, not because God takes it away from us, but because we allow a part of ourselves to die through atrophy. What has been given to us is the gift of consciousness, the ability to find joy in the persons and things that surround us, the ability to find joy in God. But our ability weakens through lack of use. Gradually, we lose our potential to experience the ordinary joys of life. In a psychological sense, we gradually die. Then our only hope is to stumble on someone or something that prods us to open our eyes.

It isn't always easy for me, my God,
to discover the importance of the pennies, nickels, and
    dimes in my life.
You know that I often look for happiness where it isn't to
    be found,
instead of looking for it where it is.
I need to look at my life with hope and love,
but those abilities need to be brought to life in me.
So I ask you to help me to see with new eyes.
I know that this is your wish too,
and so I offer this prayer with complete confidence.
Is there anything you desire more, than this—
that I should see your goodness in the many gifts that
    surround me,
and your presence within me?
Help me to experience the gift I carry within myself.

Think of some small pleasure that is a part of your every day life, and try to experience it with more attention, more awareness, and more thankfulness.

What are some of the joys of your life that you miss because you take them for granted? Do you take for granted the people who love you?

Every person carries a treasure buried within.

Jesus said that the kingdom of God is within us. God's presence is all around us, of course, but because it is everywhere, it is also at the core of our being. The joy of being awake is to discover God, not only in the people and things around us, but also deep within ourselves. This is the treasure that we carry at the center of who we are. We carry within us the presence of God, and the power to be aware of that presence. What good is the treasure, however, if we don't know how to find it? The paradox is that we'll never find it through great effort, but only by doing nothing.

Most of us have had the experience of trying to recall something we've forgotten. The harder we try to recall it, the more frustrated we become. Finally, in our frustration we stop trying. And then we remember! Sometimes the best way to recall something is to be careful not to put too much effort into it. In a parallel way, that's how we discover the presence of God within us. We have to quiet our minds, but without tying ourselves up in knots. When we allow our thoughts to come and go without grasping on to them, without paying attention to them, and without fighting to get rid of them, then our minds eventually become quiet. If we're quiet with a prayerful attitude of faith and love, we eventually become aware of the treasure we carry within. We finally come to experience what has always been there.

Quietness of mind enables us to discover God's presence not only in ourselves, but also in the world around us. We see him in others and in all of nature which flows from his hands. A lot of what we discover about God depends on our personalities. Introverts may tend to discover the presence of God within themselves. Extroverts tend to find God in the persons and things around them. We all discover what is real according to the potentials that are a part of our personalities. All of the potentials are good. But we need to balance them by trying to develop that side of us that is somewhat dormant. Introverts balance themselves by trying to notice more clearly what is outside of them. Extroverts need to increase their ability to notice God within.

The attitudes of our culture may make it difficult for us to discover the treasure within ourselves. We need a certain amount of "doing nothing" for that, but our culture often equates this with idleness. Of course, sometimes that's true. But there's another kind of "doing nothing" that enriches everything we do. A person who is quiet but lovingly conscious of the God who is everywhere may appear to be doing nothing, but looks are deceiving. A person who is lovingly conscious of God is doing something, and that internal activity affects every external action he or she does. Our interior states of mind always affect our exterior actions. A loving awareness of God gives birth to compassionate deeds. What would be the value of actions done without the inner attitude and awareness of love? That's why we always see through those who try to buy us off with material gifts while denying us the communion that is born from a caring love.

In spite of the importance of inner awareness, we sometimes feel guilty for taking creative time to be quiet, for setting aside moments to do nothing but be lovingly conscious of God. While we're taking time to do that, we wonder how we can respond to the needs of others. Perhaps the concern is more valid if it is stated the other way around. If we don't take time to become aware of God's loving presence within ourselves, how can we find the strength to respond adequately to the needs of others?

People who experience the loving presence of God within themselves discover that the love can be shared. Knowing that it is the same love of God that finds its home in every person, they see all people as their brothers and sisters. Just as the sun gives light and heat because of its inner fire, so caring people give hope and joy because of their inner love. That becomes apparent not so much in what they do, but in who they are. When we see such people, we intuitively know them as people who love. They speak to us of the fullness of what we too can be. And so, when we discover the treasure within us, we become a sign for others. That's why the presence of such people in the world is so vital for the healthy functioning of society: they are a wellspring of continuing hope.

We have two ways of loving the treasure that lies at the heart of who we are. One way is to be quietly aware of it within ourselves. The other way is to share it with others. Both ways are different experiences of the same love. Both expressions are necessary. They influence and fructify one another. For the sake of analysis, we distinguish between them, but in the whole person they eventually become one.

> "Love the Lord your God with all your heart, with all your soul, with all your strength, and with all your mind;" and "Love your neighbor as you love yourself" (Luke 10:27).

Let me not forget that I carry your presence within me,
   my God.
In the quiet of my heart, I will come to know you.
You never forget me.

May I never forget you,
for you are not only in the world around me,
but also in the depths of my heart.
Keep me patient as I strive to grow
in awareness of your presence within me.

Spend some time today talking to the God who is within you. Then be quiet for a few moments and rest in the belief that this God loves you and is present to you. You can try this when you are sitting, when you are walking, or when you are driving in your car. Be patient with this practice. Its fruits do not come all at once.

The deeper the treasure is buried, the more patience we need for the search.

No matter how well balanced and fascinating our personalities are, without patience and perseverance we never become fully awake. Patience and perseverance are the indispensable guides that lead us to the treasure within us and around us. We can't intuit the presence of God with any degree of constancy unless we develop the potential to stay awake, and that potential lies at the heart of who we are. That's part of the treasure too. But as in the development of any potential, patience and perseverance are necessary in our journey toward greater wakefulness. Without these indispensable virtues we are doomed to remain asleep.

We have to keep awake and hopeful even when it seems that there is no treasure at all. Walking in what appears to be darkness is the price we all pay for a deeper awakening to God's presence. No one can escape the experience of the darkness while waiting. That may be the reason why so often we are not prepared to wait.

Jesus told a charming story about ten bridesmaids who were waiting for the coming of the groom. Five were prepared and ready for him, and the other five were not. When the groom finally came, the unprepared ones weren't even there. Jesus pointed out the message of the story with the words, "Watch out, then, because you do not know the day or the hour" (Matthew 25:13).

Discovery of the treasure never happens according to a timetable. It never follows a well developed plan. We have no control over the moment of our awakening to God. The groom comes when we are ready, but we never know exactly when the time is ripe because there are so many unconscious barriers within us, which, of course, escape our awareness. But being ready is synonymous with being awake. We may see little of the treasure within ourselves; we may see little of the presence of God around us. But we're ready. We're awake to the possibilities of discovery through hope in God's goodness, and through the avoidance of cluttering our minds with the trivialities that put us to sleep.

So keep your eyes open, because you know neither the day nor the hour. Be patient and wait. If you keep looking with constancy, you'll grow in your ability to intuit the presence of the One who is always present to you. What appears hidden will be opened. You'll come to know the treasure within you, as well as the reflection of the God who reveals himself through his creation.

What is the secret of making this discovery? Well, it begins with faith. We begin by believing that the discovery is possible. We're not strangers to this kind of faith. Similar faith demands are made of us whenever we try to master a difficult skill. We begin by believing that we have the ability to do it.

Can you remember the first time you ever worked with a computer? This electronic marvel may have been an enigma, and a number of things you tried to do with it may not have worked at all. In the process of learning how to use the computer, it is impossible to experience how greatly it can simplify the task of writing or keeping records. The same thing happens when we try to tone up our bodies through exercise. We have to plow through the discomfort before we can experience the beneficial results. We stay with it because we have faith that the whole process is worthwhile.

In a similar way we need faith when we try to discover the treasure within ourselves. We begin by believing that God will reveal himself to us if we let him. We open ourselves to the revelation by quieting our minds, by asking God to help us see, and then by looking. Paying no attention to the thoughts in our minds, we try to become receptive to God's presence within us. Every day, we spend some time stilling our mind. We have to find our own way to do that. For some, this works best when they are sitting in a quiet place. For others, the process of quieting the mind happens best when they are walking, golfing, or working in the garden. We need to experiment to find what works best for us. When we learn to quiet our mind with faith and love, the God who is everywhere will show us who he is; or to put it in a better way, we will see what was always there to begin with. This seeing will happen, eventually, but we won't know exactly how our new state of consciousness came about. We may not understand how we become aware of God's presence within ourselves and within the world around us. When we are ready, the awareness happens, but the process remains a mystery.

Jesus illustrated this idea with the following parable:

> The Kingdom of God is like this. A man scatters seed in his field. He sleeps at night, is up and about during the

day, and all the while the seeds are sprouting and
growing. Yet he does not know how it happens. The soil
itself makes the plants grow and bear fruit; first the
tender stalk appears, then the head, and finally the head
full of grain. When the grain is ripe, the man starts
cutting it with his sickle, because harvest time has come
(Mark 4:26-29).

This is the way seeds grow. This is the way our awareness of God's presence grows. No words are adequate to
describe the process, just as there are no words to adequately describe the experience of human love. If we
want to experience human love, we must be with people
and accept them lovingly as they are. If we want to
experience God's love and presence, we must learn to
quiet our mind and pay attention prayerfully to who is
inside of us. We can have faith in the process, because it
was Jesus who said to us: "Ask, and you will receive;
seek, and you will find; knock, and the door will be
opened to you. For everyone who asks will receive, and
anyone who seeks will find, and the door will be opened
to him who knocks" (Matthew 7:7-8).

The search requires a faithful and patient heart, for the
treasure is buried deep within us and all things.

I admit that I'm often frustrated in my waiting for you,
    my God,
because I often experience so little of you.
Yet I believe that you are already here,
so how can I be waiting for you?
Is it, rather, that you are waiting for me?
You wait for me to catch on to the reality of your presence,
and I hope one day to be sufficiently awake to
    experience it.

But for now, I know you accept the degree of awareness
   I have at this moment,
because you always accept me as I am.
May I never forget that you are with me,
loving me into an ever greater awareness of who you are.
Teach me to be patient with myself,
for I haven't yet come into full bloom.

Make a commitment to persevere in paying attention to the presence of God within yourself and in the world around you. Experiment! Find your own way. You can foster your growth in awareness of God's presence by doing reflective spiritual reading. Read a bit and then let the Spirit speak within you. When your mind begins to wander, read a bit more. Keep repeating the process. As time goes on, the periods of silence will grow. If you need vocal prayer, you can pray the rosary, pausing in silence between the decades so that you can listen to the Spirit. A walk outdoors may also reveal the Spirit's presence to you.

Experiment and be patient with your journey toward awareness. Believe that God loves you and that God wants you to be aware of his presence in your daily life. Believe this even when it seems to you that God is absent.

A bud becomes a flower only in its own time.

A mark of wisdom is the ability to accept yourself as you are. God does. God knows that, at this given moment, we cannot be other than we are. Perhaps most of us are buds which haven't matured yet. The best is yet to come. If we can't be content with that, we'll have to live with a lot of unnecessary psychological and spiritual discomfort.

God doesn't want that for us. In the face of all your expectations for yourself and your desire to grow, what would it mean to accept yourself as you are?

The Japanese have a saying: "Seven times down; eight times up. That's the way life is." Jesus put a different slant on it when he said that we should forgive each other not only seven times, but seventy times seven. That too seems to flow from the way life is. But wouldn't this also apply to the necessity of forgiving ourselves? Most of us fall often. If we spend too much energy disliking ourselves because of our falls, where will we get enough energy to get up and go on? Accepting ourselves as we are would mean acknowledging our shadow side, avoiding unproductive regret, and believing that we are loveable even in our failures. Perhaps at the present moment, God is more interested in how patient we are with ourselves, rather than in how perfect we've become. There's a time to examine ourselves and to be open to change, but there's also a time to accept ourselves as wounded people who haven't yet come to full bloom.

Accepting ourselves with all of our weaknesses is a way of standing humbly before God. That's extremely hard to do, and many people have to struggle to do it. To complicate matters, much of the struggle takes place on the unconscious level, sometimes affecting us in ways that escape our conscious awareness. Because of our failures, we may be hostile toward ourselves and not even know it. But sooner or later, our bodies catch on. They sometimes react with illness, which offers us a reflection of what is going on within our minds and hearts.

Self-acceptance wouldn't be possible for us at all if we allowed our egos to dominate the way we think. It's the ego that gets bruised by our shortcomings and honest self-evaluations. It's the ego that makes us miserable by telling us that we're never quite good enough, and it's the ego that makes accepting our failures so difficult. That's why every major religion carries a similar message about the ego, telling us that it needs to be put on a diet, so to speak. We can stop feeding the ego by admitting not only our strengths but also our shadows, and by loving ourselves and others as God does. Love and a healthy self-acceptance reduce our egos to their proper proportions. Then they become our friends instead of our masters.

Would self-acceptance have anything to do with our relationships to others? Jesus told us to love others as we love ourselves. What would happen in our relationships if we refused to accept ourselves? Would we be able to accept another person's shadows if we couldn't accept our own? If we are put off by other people's weaknesses, how will we ever get close enough to discover their strengths? Perhaps those most capable of love are the ones who can look at a bud and intuit the possibilities of the flower. The intuition, however, begins with ourselves.

Would our acceptance of our imperfections influence the way in which we relate to God? Doesn't it seem that God's revelation in space and time also has its own shadow side that calls for our acceptance? Being tolerant of our own imperfections, we would be able to accept the imperfections we find in creation. Nature, beautiful as it is, often plagues us with its shadow side. Some of our sufferings come from nature itself. We suffer from bacterial and viral illnesses, from drought, from genetic malfunctioning. It is hard to see how we are always responsible for these kinds of sufferings. Although God does not cause these sufferings, they are a part of the world that he sustains. Otherwise, they wouldn't exist. The problem of suffering that we seem not to cause is the mystery that engaged the writer of the book of Job. After all of his pondering, the mystery remained what it must always be, a mystery. The final answer of Jesus to the

problem of suffering, the shadow-side of life, is the resurrection. But in the meantime, will we be able to accept life
as it is and as it has to be, not letting its shadows dull the
vision of the beauty that is its gift? Our life now is like a
bud. Eventually it will become like the flower. The
present and the future—we live with mystery on both
ends. Will we have sufficient faith and love to accept the
shadows of our present life, even though we can't understand them?

While accepting the shadows, don't forget to notice the
light. Along with our weaknesses, there is much good
within us. In the midst of other people's frailties, there can
be magnificent strengths. In the midst of life's imperfections, there is great beauty which reveals itself to those
who are awake. Awareness of the positive aspects of life
makes it easier to accept the shadows. Finally, we learn to
intuit the presence of the flower by looking at the bud.

Complete acceptance of what we cannot change is the
foundation for discovering the treasure within us, and the
presence of God around us. Accepting life that is never
perfect, accepting ourselves as buds that haven't flowered
yet, these are the psycho-spiritual infrastructures that support a life of deeper consciousness. How could we grow
in consciousness of God's presence in our lives if our
attention were focused on our dissatisfactions with ourselves or with others? When we focus too much of our
energies on the negative aspects of life, we squander our
opportunities for deeper consciousness. We need to accept
that we, along with the rest of life, are simply in the
budding stage, that the flower is yet to come. And that's
OK, because for this present moment, life can't be any
different than it is. When we accept this, we are free to go
beyond our egos and to reach for the stars. We all have to
find our own way to remove the blocks in ourselves that
keep this vision from sustaining our lives.

God, you know my impatience.
Your concept of time is quite different from my own,
and in your patience, you accept the buds of life,
knowing that the flowers will come in their own time.
I have a difficulty with my own slowness to change,
and it's hard for me to accept the imperfections of others.
I even have a problem with the imperfections of life itself,
and all of this blinds me to your presence.
I need to be able to see myself and others as you do.
My ego stands in the way, my God.
I ask for the strength to be free from my own
    narrow vision,
that I might see with yours.
May I find a way to eliminate the blocks that keep me from
    accepting life as it is,
the blocks that keep me from finding you where you are
    to be found.

The next time you do not succeed at something as well as you might wish, be gentle with yourself. Be patient with yourself as God is patient with you. The next time members of your family or of your community do not succeed at something as well as you might wish, be gentle with them. Be patient with them as God is patient with you. Remember that they, as well as you, are not yet in full bloom. Remember too that impatience absorbs your energy, leaving you with less energy to live fully in the present moment.

To become fully conscious, we need to discover God not only within ourselves, but also within community.

The righteous will then answer him, "When, Lord, did we ever see you hungry and feed you, or thirsty and give you a drink?" The King will reply, "I tell you, whenever you did this for one of the least important of these brothers or sisters of mine, you did it for me!" (Matthew 25:37, 40).

Our journey toward consciousness is not exclusively between God and ourselves. The journey includes all of our brothers and sisters. The Bible makes it clear in many different ways that love is not divisible. Not only are we all children of God, but we also quite literally carry within us the very life of God. It is this life that makes us one. The divine life is the same in all of us. Realizing this, we are impelled even more deeply to love and to care for one another. People unaware of the beauty and of the needs of their brothers and sisters travel though life with a consciousness that is not fully awake. They remain isolated from much of what is real. No one discovers the full significance of what it means to be conscious without a loving awareness of others.

Consciousness of others grows through friendship, which enables us to experience more concretely the give and take of love. The attraction of friendship teaches us about the beauty of other personalities. Paying attention to others, we uncover the magnificence of human qualities that would escape us if we were unaware of the people who reveal them to us. Here is another example of how much joy is lost if we choose to remain unconscious!

Paradoxically, friendship takes us out of ourselves, and yet at the same time enables us to discover something about ourselves. In loving our friends and paying attention to them, we learn something about who we are. When we are loyal to our friends, we discover our capacity to be faithful. When we put ourselves out for our friends, we discover our capacity for self sacrifice. When our friends love us, we discover that we are loveable. And when men and women reach out in friendship to one another, they discover more deeply their masculine and feminine identities which make them to be who they are.

Consciousness of others also grows through service, a ministering to the needs of others that is born of compassion. Compassionate service comes from the realization of our own suffering. Knowing our own sufferings, we are able to become aware of the sufferings of others. Of course, it is possible to preoccupy ourselves with our own sufferings and refuse to respond to the needs of others. We can choose to live without consciousness of others and be locked up within ourselves. This is an unfortunate choice, of course, for it leads to a devastating restriction of awareness. Our own sufferings become worse because we center our conscious energy on ourselves instead of directing it to others. Perhaps we have all experienced how much worse our worries, fears, and other problems become when we allow ourselves to become overly preoccupied with them.

Finally, our consciousness of others grows through prayer, prayer with others and prayer for others. People who prayerfully share their spiritual journeys are united in friendship on the deepest level possible, for they become aware of God as their common bond. A beautiful example of this shines out in the story of the two disciples on their way to Emmaus (Luke 24:13-35). As they share with each other their confusion and disappointment about the death of Jesus, a stranger appears to them. He sheds light on the meaning of Jesus' death and resurrection, and then breaks bread with them. In the breaking of the bread, the eyes of the disciples are opened, and they recognize the Lord. After this prayer experience, Jesus leaves, and the disciples share the joy they experienced in his presence. Their common bond is Jesus. Their consciousness of this bond deepens not only their awareness of God, but also their awareness of each other. If we have had these kinds of experience with our friends, we can easily understand how they lead us to a deeper understanding of love.

We pray not only with others, but also for others. Praying for others teaches us compassion as well as our mutual dependence on one another, and ultimately, our dependence upon God. We count on one another's prayers, because through prayer come the gifts of solidarity and strength. We count on God's response to prayer because through his care come the added gifts of divine love and peace. Hoping for these gifts, we discover that we are all interdependent. Our awareness is meant to fly beyond the concerns of the individual ego that it might embrace all.

I want to remember, my God, that when you come to me,
you bring all of my brothers and sisters with you.
How could it be otherwise?
They are constantly in your mind and in your love.
You carry them with you always.
If I don't love them, how can I love you?
If I am unconscious of them, how shall I ever be more fully
  conscious of you?
Teach me the difficult lesson of love, my God,
so that I won't be left with just myself.

May my awareness of love grow,
that I might experience oneness with you
and with all those whom your love has called into being.

Reflect on the bonds that unite you to those you love. Remember the shared experiences that have entwined your life with those of your family and friends. Ask yourself if you deeply appreciate the love of your friends and family, or if you simply take their love for granted. Ask too if you are faithful in showing compassion toward the poor and the suffering who need your concern and your help.

TWO

Gateways to a Fully Conscious Life

The young woman asked the teacher, "What can I do to develop my awareness of life?"

The teacher replied, "Pay attention to the way you think, the way you believe, and the way you act. Right thinking, right believing, and right acting are the gateways to the joys of deeper awareness. Choose to enter these gateways. It is a choice for life."

> The scriptures say: "I am now giving you the choice between life and death, between God's blessing and God's curse, and I call heaven and earth to witness the choice you make. Choose life."
>
> —Deuteronomy 30:19

Without a desire for consciousness, we make
the choice to remain only half alive.

People wake up and become more deeply conscious to
the extent that they are eager for life. Notice the way an
alert child responds to life. An inborn curiosity impels a
child to experience as much of her environment as she
can take in. A child notices and touches almost everything. A child's response to life involves her whole being.
Isn't there something we can learn from a healthy child's
eagerness for life? An alert, loving and holistic involvement with life is the main gateway to consciousness.

Somewhere along our life's journey we lose that sense
of total involvement that characterizes a child. Life loses
its mystery for us and we are content simply to live in our
heads. We substitute thought and concepts for experience,
something that results in part from our educational sys-
tem. In the process, we sometimes lose contact with the
reality around us. Once we become eager for a holistic
experience that includes both our heads and our hearts,
the possibility of deeper awareness dawns for us. The
depth of our consciousness is determined by the depth of
our desire to experience a positive feeling for life.

What is the depth of your desire to be conscious of the
beauty of life? Do you walk in the fields or among the
trees? Do you look at your surroundings and often miss
the beauty? Do you miss the presence of the creator in
what surrounds you? How desirous are you of knowing
the loving presence of the God who is always within you,
closer to you than you are to yourself? How strong is
your wish to become more aware of the love that your
relatives and friends carry for you? And how potent is
your desire to know yourself more deeply, to come to a
more complete realization of who you are? Consciousness is the result of an eager curiosity to experience all of

life at a deeper level. Without this eager curiosity, no deeper awareness can develop.

How does such a curiosity grow? When we become aware of the different possibilities of being conscious, an eagerness for a deeper awareness can begin to stir within us. The process begins when we open our eyes. When we discover someone or something attractive, we are ready to explore who or whatever it is that draws us. If we do not squelch the eagerness, it leads us to become more awake, and then we become hooked! So it is with all of our life experiences.

The journey of consciousness begins with an act of faith that there is much more to life than we imagine. When the act of faith leads to an actual experience, then a deeper sensitivity to the reality within and around us comes into play. We begin to be where we are, and to notice what is here. We plunge into the journey of discovering in our lives what had always been present and yet unnoticed, because we were asleep. And when we finally wake up, we wonder where we have been all of our lives!

I'm not sure what these deeper levels of consciousness
    might be like, my God.
I want to believe that there is more to the
    experience of life
than my usual state of awareness has led me to believe.
I've often been lost in peripheral concerns,
and, yes, sometimes I've just been plain bored.
Maybe you'd find that comical.
There's so much to experience in life, yet I'm often
    asleep to it.

Increase my eagerness to experience life,
and give me a deeper faith in life's possibilities.
Remove from my mind and heart all of the dross
that keeps me from being fully alive
   and fully conscious.

How much enthusiasm do you have for your life? When you wake up in the morning, do you believe that your day can be an adventure of consciousness? The more you believe in this possibility, the more you will be able to rid yourself of the heaviness that keeps you from experiencing your life with eagerness and joy.

The price of fuller consciousness is the positive purification of the mind and heart.

The reason some of us fail to become fully conscious is because of our tendency toward self-centeredness. We misuse our energies on things that oftentimes do not mean much. As a result, the gateways to consciousness become blocked for us. Positive purification of the mind and heart requires us to direct our conscious energies toward things that matter, rather than toward things that do not. Positive purification means a firm direction toward compassion and oneness with others, rather than toward indifference or an unhealthy preoccupation with ourselves. It means accomplishing what is good, and avoiding what is hurtful both to others and to ourselves.

Without purification, no significant deepening of conscious awareness can take place. An unpurified mind simply remains stuck within itself. The ego of an unpurified mind absorbs all of the mind's energies like a black hole swallowing up light. The unpurified ego captures our energies and absorbs them, trapping them within itself. The greater the ego, the greater the trap. The ego ends up without much conscious energy left to expend on anything other than itself, and so the egoist is largely unconscious. It would seem only logical, then, that the life of unrelenting egoism would be a life of perfect boredom.

Are you sufficiently purified for the great adventure of becoming more conscious? You only know through an honest self- examination, something that needs to be done at regular intervals. When you discover that your energies are becoming trapped within yourself rather than moving outward toward others, you know that you need to change directions.

Human nature almost always remains prone to the double trap of selfishness and pettiness, illusory ways of living that keep people from becoming fully awake. An unpurified mind is like a stagnant pond that has no water flowing in or out. Gradually it putrefies. A mind stuck in itself slowly dies to anything that lies outside of its own narrow parameters, and so its ability to be loving and joyful is lost. This condition of human nature is part of what Christians mean by original sin. Buddhists call this condition ignorance, *avidya*. Until we learn how to come out of this state, we are in a situation of egoism which causes much of our suffering. Since egoism locks us within ourselves, egoism keeps us from seeing and experiencing reality in its broader aspects. It is egoism, the result of an unpurified mind and heart, that keeps us from being fully conscious.

The story is told of a boy who needed glasses. The world appeared fuzzy to him, but he thought this was just the normal state of things. He never knew he needed glasses until one day his parents took him to an optometrist. After he was fitted with corrective lenses, a whole new world of vision opened up to him. He had no idea that people and things could look so clear and sharp. Purifying the mind and heart by rooting out excessive concern with ourselves is like going to the optometrist. We begin to understand that our minds and hearts can be put into better focus. Only then can we successfully begin the journey into deeper consciousness.

Purifying the mind through a positive moral life and getting the mind back in focus are the tasks of a person who wants to become more deeply conscious. This direction of our energies outward can either take the form of active service suitable to our life circumstances, or it can take the form of prayer for others. Both service and prayer are aspects of love that make us more conscious of our communion with other people.

The process of purifying the mind and heart is an ongoing one that usually requires a good deal of effort. Through continuing faith and diligent purification of the mind and heart, we prepare the fertile soil in which a deeper state of consciousness can take root within ourselves and come to fruition.

I freely admit to you, my God,

that I have a great need to be purified

of the many forms of egoism that defile my life.

What I ask from you is the light of your spirit.

I need to understand how I might better respond to your
will for me

by becoming more like you.

Give me the courage and love to become less preoccupied
with myself,

so that I might become more conscious of the needs of
those around me.

Make an honest inventory of your thoughts and actions. Is there a preoccupation with your needs and desires that keeps you from being aware of God's presence? In what way do you need to make a better response to the will of God for you, along with a better response to the needs of others?

*P*urification of the mind and heart is impossible without self-awareness.

A morbid kind of self-awareness leads to egoism and perhaps even to physical and psychological illness. An enlightened kind of self-awareness leads to the knowledge that we are lovable as well as selfish. When we are aware of our selfishness, we can, with the help of God's power within us, cleanse ourselves of it.

Charles Dickens' tale about Ebenezer Scrooge in *A Christmas Carol* is a story of purification or healing through self-awareness. As you may remember, Scrooge's miserly selfishness nearly destroyed the life of his underpaid employee, Bob Cratchit, as well as the lives of Cratchit's family. In the process, Scrooge made his own life miserable. Until a series of dreams made it clear to him, Scrooge was not fully conscious of the negative results of his actions, nor fully conscious of how his actions were causing his own misery. It was the new self-knowledge gained from his dreams that freed him from selfishness and enabled him to care for others. In the process of waking up, he became quite a different person with a much deeper level of awareness than he possessed before the dream. Without the new self-awareness, there would have been no change. Scrooge simply would have remained asleep to many of the finer possibilities of his life.

We may not always have the benefit of dream knowledge, although if we know how to interpret the dreams we have, we might learn quite a lot. But we can have the benefit of intelligent self-awareness. Reflecting honestly on our lives, we come to see which attitudes and actions contribute to our happiness and which ones do not.

Usually, our growth in self-awareness is helped along through the insights of others who assist us to see ourselves as we are. Scrooge was helped by his former partner Marley, who appeared to him in a dream. In our quest for self-knowledge, we can be helped by others who know and love us. Others are able to see things in us that we sometimes miss. Who has not experienced this? It is sometimes a painful experience, but a profitable one for growth. Relatives, friends, and counselors may be willing to accompany us on our journey toward self-awareness, if we allow them to. They can help us to see both our strengths and our weaknesses. If there are such persons in our lives, they are allies in our search to become more conscious and more alive. They are a gift. Perhaps all that is necessary is that we become humble enough to seek them out.

Get to know yourself. Become aware of your attitudes about your work, about people whom you love, about people whom you find it difficult to love. Become aware of your attitudes about your life, about the importance of compassion in your life, about the importance of leisure without which you never become fully conscious. Become aware of your attitude toward God, the reality that underlies everything else in your life. Become aware of the depth of your desire to become more awake. Of course, this is a big order. If you don't know these things about yourself, though, you may risk living with illusions that thwart your potential to be more responsive to others, more deeply conscious. When your illusions are brought to light, they lose much of their ability to harm you. Unmask them, and, like Scrooge in the Christmas story, you become more aware of the people and things around you, more able to respond with care to their needs.

You know me, my God.

You know how I shrink from the experience of fully knowing myself,

because there are some things about myself that I'd rather not know.

And then, sometimes, the whole process just seems like a waste of time.

I'd rather be doing something else.

Give me the courage to confront myself calmly,

the courage to allow others to help me in my quest for self-knowledge.

May I learn to take time for those things in my life that are important,

and to let go of some of the hyperactivity in my life

that only serves to dull my consciousness.

Find a clergy person, a counselor, or a friend with whom you can make an evaluation of your life, especially from the point of view of your openness to others. If you're not quite ready to do this, at least be open to the possibility. Others can be of great help to you as you proceed on the journey of self-discovery. It is important to allow time in your life to get the help you need.

Without leisure in our lives, we never become fully conscious.

Earlier cultures had their own particular ways of finding their leisure. Some civilizations used slaves to free their citizens from the constant drudgery of work. The Old Testament had a much better solution. The Jews consecrated the seventh day of the week to the Lord. On that day there was to be no work at all, only the leisure to rest their minds. That gave them the freedom to become more aware of another dimension of their lives that otherwise might have been compromised. In our culture, many people refuse to make time for leisure. Others use the time, but they often fritter it away in front of the television set, which sometimes just serves to make them more unconscious. It is the creative use of leisure, however, which is an indispensable element in opening the gateways of consciousness. Leisure helps us to become more alive.

Two friends take a few moments at the end of the day to sit and have coffee together. One friend looks at the other and asks how she spent her day.

"Oh, I had a really profitable day," she said. "I sold a house for three hundred thousand dollars. Can you imagine what a commission that will bring? And then I hired another fantastic salesperson for our agency. We'll probably be doing more business than any other agency in town. Oh, and I finished the plans for Dolores' surprise birthday party. What did you do today?"

"Oh," her friend replied, "I was in the garden for several hours, and then, I read for an hour or so. After that, I don't know. I just let myself be."

Her friend looked at her quizzically.

Consciousness has a lot to do with what happens when you just let yourself be. For many in our culture, that would seem like a waste of time. The first woman in the story may have seemed to us to be more fully alive to us than the second one, but that could be a false perception. The mind that learns to be quiet and perceptive is the one that has the best chance of becoming more conscious, more alive. We need leisure. We need quiet periods. Without them, we never learn how to be calmly perceptive in the midst of our daily activities. And without a calm, quiet mind, we are more likely to become upset and preoccupied with the noise that goes on within our egos. It's the noise in our egos that keeps us from being fully conscious. Could you appreciate your favorite kind of music if it were half-drowned out by static?

The noise and static in our everyday lives are our worries, our preoccupations with the future, our fears, and our unfulfilled desires. Unless the mind frees itself from them and becomes quiet, we cannot live fully in the present moment. It is when we take time just to be that we learn how to quiet the mind. Leisure is imperative. How else do we learn to get rid of the static?

For those still concerned about productivity, they should know that a quiet mind is their best ally in becoming productive. When people bring a quiet, concentrated mind to what they are doing, more gets done. People who meditate can learn to preserve a quiet mind even in the midst of noise. Not only do their leisure moments become more creative, but their productive moments become more productive. Haven't you noticed that when your mind is not distracted, you accomplish more?

How does one develop a quiet mind? Well, would you believe that one can learn to do this simply by being quiet? A person develops a muscular body by doing certain kinds of exercises. Exercise is the key. A person develops a quiet mind by creatively doing nothing. Leisure is the key. It is hard to say whether exercise or leisure is more difficult. It would seem, though, that a person could learn to enjoy doing either one.

Some people feel guilty when they take leisure time for themselves. It seems to them that nothing is being accomplished. But the greatest accomplishment of any human being is to become more conscious, more aware, more perceptive, and therefore more alive. Of course, we have to prove this to ourselves. What about you? Would you be willing to taste the experience of creatively doing nothing? Would you be willing to take a walk and just see what you see, just hear what you hear? Would you be willing to turn on some music, and not just have it as background noise, but really listen to it? And finally, would you be willing to play, or perhaps simply be quiet, and just enjoy the feeling of being fully alive? The joy of fuller consciousness can only come from a life that has some leisure in it. Creative leisure brings in its wake a calmer, more peaceful experience of life. Both mind and body benefit. A calm, relaxed mind influences the body and increases its health. A calm, relaxed body influences the mind and increases its consciousness.

Jesus once said to his disciples, who had been exhausted by the demands of others, "Let us go off by ourselves to some place where we will be alone and you can rest a while" (Mark 6:31). An invitation to rest when there was still so much to do! Are you ready for that?

My God, may my mind not become numb in the midst of
    all my daily activities.
You put within me a natural rhythm that seeks a balance
    between activity and rest.
May I not become so out of touch with myself
that I lose this sense of balance.

I want to preserve myself from the excessive levels of
activity
that would keep me from becoming more fully conscious.
I think this is what you would wish me to do, my God.
Help me to do it
that I might have greater health in my body and in
my mind.

Take time to do something enjoyable that you have
wanted to do, something that you have denied to yourself
because of a supposed lack of time. This is especially
important when the hectic pace of life makes you overly
tense. Experiment with different ways to relax your mind
and your body. Experiment with different forms of recrea-
tion that will bring your mind and your body back into a
state of better balance.

Fully conscious people always make their bodies allies of their minds.

There was a time when, in some forms of spirituality,
the body did not count for much. St. Bernard of Clairvaux is said to have mortified his body so much that he
developed severe stomach problems. The story is told
that the monks of his monastery provided a receptacle
next to his choir stall. Thus, if it became necessary for him
to regurgitate, he could do so in his place without having
to leave the church. This probably did little to enhance
the celebration of vespers at Clairvaux, but St. Bernard
did warn his monks not to follow his example in defying
the body.

Contemporary spiritual writers tell us not to forget our
bodies in our journey toward consciousness. Our bodies

are our allies. It seems strange to suppose that our minds and bodies might be at odds with each other. We are our minds and bodies. They are simply two sides of the coin. It is as mind/body persons that we become conscious. If either the mind or the body were missing, we would not be conscious at all. And so, as we journey toward fuller consciousness in all of its forms, it would seem wise to let our bodies become allies of our minds.

Calm your body before you meditate. Sit with your spine erect, feet flat on the floor. This helps to put your body in a state of relaxed alertness. When the body is relaxed and alert, it becomes an ally of the mind. If you sit in a slouching position with your legs crossed, your body soon becomes restless. Its muscles clamor to be moved and your body quickly ceases to be an effective ally of a mind which is trying to become calm. In meditation, the body's position is crucial. At the very least, try to find a position that keeps your body comfortable and alert.

As you begin to meditate, pay attention to your breathing, to the natural rhythm of the breath as it flows in and out of you. Doing this with the body helps to relax the mind. The experience of relaxation that comes from this is similar to what happens when you listen to the rhythmic breaking of the waves on a seashore. Listening to the repetition of the sound puts you in a relaxed state. Certain sounds are helpful for the deepening of consciousness, while others are distracting. Put yourself in a situation where the sounds are helpful, or if you prefer, try to put yourself in a situation where there are hardly any sounds at all. As you breathe, listen to the sound of your breathing and feel its rhythm. Then as you quiet your mind, your body becomes your ally, working with you to create an experience of peace and receptivity.

You can make your body an ally when you sit quietly

in your room and meditate, or when you sit outside and simply observe anything beautiful that captures your attention. As you relax your body and mind, you have a greater possibility of feeling a kind of unity with what you observe. Putting away all thoughts from your mind, you discover that your perceptions become sharper, and that what you observe slowly becomes a part of you.

You can allow your body to work harmoniously with you when you stand. If you stand erect with the center of gravity within the abdominal region, if you stand firmly on both feet without slouching against the wall, your mind will be more centered. You will be more attentive, more perceptive of what is going on around you.

You can make your body an ally even in the midst of your activities. Most of the things that effect the mind also effect the body. Mind and body always influence each other. Be attentive to your body as you work or play, and notice where the areas of tension are. Many times the body is tense and we are unaware of it, and so there isn't much that can be done to alleviate the tension. When you become aware of your physical tensions, it is possible to relax the tensions away, even while you are working. If the tensions are more severe, progressive relaxation techniques can be a help. Several books have been written explaining how progressive relaxation techniques work. You can also try to understand where the tensions are coming from. The body records the activities of the mind. If the mind is tense, the body finds a way to mirror the tenseness. When you reflect on your daily life, you may discover the causes of the tensions. With honest reflection, you may discover the presence of resentments and dissatisfactions that translate themselves into uncomfortable physical stress. Tensions are the results of your body trying to communicate with you. Listen to what it has to say. If you pay attention to it, you may be able to set yourself free, not only from the tensions, but also from their causes. A calm body is the ally of a calm mind, but it takes work on your part to create the harmonious relationship.

If you really love your body, show it that you care. Feed it nourishing food. If you feed it junk, eventually it will no longer by your ally. Exercise it. Its muscles were meant to move, and that's what they like to do. If you avoid exercising it, it will spread its lethargy to your mind. Give your body adequate rest and it will help your mind to be more alive and awake. Run it into the ground and it will try to put your mind to sleep.

The body is an integral part of your journey toward consciousness, toward the God who is within you. Make it your ally as you progress on your journey. If you are like the majority of the human race, you need all the help you can get. It makes sense, then, to enlist the help of your body, because, after all, your body is you. And in your deepest states of conscious awareness, in your deepest states of union with God, your body and mind are one.

> Don't you know your body is the temple of the Holy Spirit, who lives in you and who was given to you by God? You do not belong to yourselves but to God; he bought you for a price. So use your bodies for God's glory (1 Corinthians 6:19-20).

I am a gift of your love, my God,
I, and my brothers and sisters.
My body is a gift of your love,
without which I would not even be conscious.
Help me to appreciate and to care for this gift,
to understand it and to make it my ally

as I open up my whole being to you.
May I be faithful to you on every level of my being.

Close your eyes, sit in a quiet place and pay attention to the movement of your breath. Gently put all other thoughts out of your mind, being attentive only to the rhythm of your breathing. Notice how, after some minutes, this physical experience begins to quiet your mind.

Learn to identify areas of tension within your body. Relax those areas and try to identify the reasons why those tensions arose.

Treat your body with respect. Give it the rest, exercise, and healthful nourishment it deserves, so that it will be a worthy ally in your journey toward consciousness.

> *The light of full consciousness dawns only*
> *in those who are faithful to*
> *staying awake in the darkness.*

God created us to be lovingly conscious of our brothers and sisters, and of everything that God has made and of God's very self. We are created in the image of the One who is the absolute fullness of consciousness. Full human consciousness is our birthright, though we never achieve it without a struggle. When we have become as completely conscious as we can, then we are most fully ourselves. To be lovingly aware and awake is God's will for us. The following text from scripture bears this out.

> A teacher of the Law came up and tried to trap Jesus. "Teacher," he asked, "what must I do to receive eternal life?"

> Jesus answered him, "What do the scriptures say? How do you interpret them?"
>
> The man answered, "'Love the Lord your God with all your heart, with all your soul, with all your strength, and with all your mind'; and 'Love your neighbor as you love yourself.'"
>
> "You are right," Jesus replied; "do this and you will live" (Luke 10:25-28).

Fulfilling this command means more than obeying God's will by acting morally toward others. It means being fully and lovingly conscious of God's presence within ourselves and within everything God has made. Could there be any real love without that kind of awareness? From the depths of loving consciousness comes our response of service. Consciousness and response reinforce one another. When their interaction in our lives takes place within the milieu of love, we become more awake to God and to our brothers and sisters. Faithfulness to God is our faithfulness to this process of integral awareness, even when loving becomes difficult and we seem to walk in darkness. This faithfulness is also a faithfulness to ourselves, to what God has made us to be.

If our lives are permeated by fidelity, we will persevere in our journey toward full consciousness in spite of all the obstacles that are a part of the journey. Overcoming the indifference and the doubts that so often darken the journey, we will progressively develop a taste for being fully alive. We will notice a passion developing within ourselves, a passion for being awake, for being fully conscious. Passion for consciousness is the mark of a person who is becoming more awake, and pre-eminently it is the mark of God in whose image we are made.

Growth in consciousness comes as God's gift to us. While we need to prepare for it by trying to stay awake to all of the ways in which God reveals himself, our efforts alone do not guarantee success. The actual deepening of consciousness is a gift of God that we never quite fully understand. If we trust in the gift, we can weather the difficulties and darkness that are a part of the journey toward more conscious life. We simply remain faithful to the promise and the mystery. How it all unfolds is determined by the wisdom of God which is beyond our comprehension. In this sense, we are left somewhat in the dark, and we have to rely on the light of faith as our journey unfolds. This is always important to remember when we experience darkness and difficulties along the journey toward deeper love and deeper life.

Our fidelity to prayer and to growth in consciousness is proven by our ability to persevere through different experiences of darkness. A young woman once said to me, "There was a six month period in my life when I hated to see my husband come home. I knew I would have to cook something for him, and I hated the thought of that." The dark period did finally pass, and the young woman learned an important truth that we all eventually come to experience. Affections sometimes wane. Dark and dry periods are a part of every relationship. We experience them with persons we love; we experience them with God. Rather than lose heart in the darkness, we need to remain faithful, awake and watchful for the return of the light. Without this attitude of faith, we cannot grow in consciousness.

There are dark periods in our lives that come from our being out of tune with God, and there are dark periods that just come, apparently for no reason at all. Both kinds of darkness are a gift. The first kind is a gift because it tells us that something is amiss with our lives. When we discover what needs healing, we can, with the power of God, bring ourselves back to wholeness. The second kind is a gift because the darkness teaches us to be faithful to love, not because we get some kind of personal satisfaction from our faithfulness, but simply because we love the other. The darkness purifies us and develops selfless love, provided we are willing to persevere in faith. Our faith is the indispensable element in our journey toward consciousness, and yet, even our ability to be faithful is God's gift to us.

I have scattered my life energies on so many peripheral
    things, my God.
And yet you have created me to experience you,
you who alone are truly real.
At the core of my being, you wait for me to discover you.
In everyone and everything around me you wait for me to
    find you.
I know that this is your will for me.
And yet, sometimes, you seem so far away.
It's at those times, my God, when my faith seems to
    stumble.
I need your strength to weather the darkness.
Whatever its reason or its purpose,
may the darkness not cause me to abort my journey
    toward you,
and toward my brothers and sisters.
I rely on you to keep me faithful to the journey
and to the call that you place in my heart.

Recall a period of darkness or crisis in your life. How did your faith and reliance on God's strength help you out of it? To what extent does your faith enable you to persevere through the dark moments of your life? To what extent does your faith enable you to experience the presence of God's loving care in a more personal way? Have you encouraged others to have faith in the midst of their own difficult moments?

God reveals his personal presence to those who relate to him on a personal level.

It would be a mistake to suppose that God is some kind of a divine object located somewhere in the distance outside of ourselves. God is within us and all around us, not as an object that we reach out to, but as a personal presence in whom we are immersed. St. Paul expressed this beautifully when he said, "Yet God is actually not far from any one of us; as someone has said, 'In him we live and move and exist'" (Acts 17:27-28). God, then, is not a particular being to whom we can point, but rather a personal presence that permeates all there is. That is why God is both within us and all around us. God is the personal milieu in which we live.

To say that God is personal is to say that God is interested in us. It is to say that God deeply loves us and that he desires our happiness. God's personal communication comes to us through his word in Jesus Christ. It comes to us through the inspirations of his Spirit within us. It comes to us through the daily strength we receive from God to cope with our lives. It comes to us through silence. To become conscious of the true God is to become conscious of the God who cares. Nowhere did Jesus verbally express God's care and concern more intimately than in chapters 14-17 of John's gospel. Nowhere did he show his care and concern for us more beautifully than in his death and resurrection.

The care and concern of our God can only be known by

those who personally relate to God's presence and God's revelation. It is through our fully human interaction with God that we learn to experience that God is one who cares deeply about us and shares our journey toward consciousness with us. We experience a similar dynamic in our relationships with one another. A friend's love only becomes meaningful to us when we relate to the love, returning his or her love with our own.

The most significant thrust we can make in our journey toward consciousness is to become more aware that God's presence is always personal. According to the particular personality we have, we need to find our own way of developing this awareness. One very beautiful way to develop this is to communicate silently with God throughout the day, much in the same way that one might say things to a friend. The communication is about what is happening in the present moment. We communicate thankfulness in the midst of what is beautiful, or make a cry for help in the midst of what is difficult. It would seem possible to talk to God about anything that would be on our minds at any given moment. Slowly, this kind of communication helps us to realize that God shares everything about our lives. Eventually, as this realization develops, we experience that in some way, we and God are one.

For other people, the communication more readily takes place in the form of a mantra, a short prayer consisting of a few words that can be repeated again and again. The first step is to find a short prayer or mantra that strikes us as meaningful. It is important to experiment until we find one that seems appropriate. An example that comes from the eastern Christian tradition is, "Lord Jesus Christ, have mercy on me a sinner." There are many possibilities, but once we find one that fits, it is best to stick with it. The whole point of this kind of prayer is to quiet the mind and to make us more aware that God is very much with us, very much a personal reality within our life. If we constantly change the form of the prayer, its effectiveness in quieting our mind may be diminished.

Traditional prayer offers another way for many people to encounter the personal God who loves them. All prayer is meant to awaken us to the loving presence of God both within ourselves and within others. It is a powerful means for putting our lives in tune with God. If these results come from the prayers we say, then those prayers are an indispensable part of our journey toward consciousness. The motivation for saying these prayers will be the desire to grow in love and oneness. Once we have experienced this growth, we will be less likely to fall into a routine or merely to pray from a sense of duty. The motivation will be more personal.

Serving the needs of others is another essential way to realize the personal presence of God. In serving the needs of others with love, we do what God does, and so we come to know God through what we do. Since God is personally present in an intimate way to each person, what we do to another person we do to God. This makes sense only if we believe that God identifies himself with each one of us. Sometimes people of deep prayer discover this truth experientially. They experience quite clearly that God actually is one with all of his people. Most of us have to accept this oneness in faith, while hoping that one day we will actually know this oneness as a personal experience. Perhaps our compassion for others will gradually lead us to a deeper realization of the unity that we all share in God.

Finally, it is in the depths of silence that we come to experience the presence of our personal God. In silence, we come to know that we are loved and that we are one. People who love one another deeply understand this well. In silent awareness, they speak to one another simply by their presence. This is what we can hope to experience in our silent relationship with God. It is an experience that will escape us unless we are willing to make room in our lives for silence. This is crucial. Silent prayer often teaches us about the personal presence of God in ways that words and activities never can.

A good way to prepare for the experience of silent prayer is to read a short passage of scripture and actively reflect on it. After the reflection is made, one praises God for his goodness and then rests for a few moments in silence, listening for the Spirit's prompting deep within the heart. One speaks personally to God and then listens for God's response. If nothing seems to come, one reads a little more and then repeats the process of reflection and listening. Eventually, the periods of silence may tend to lengthen. Whatever happens, it is important to experiment, to find our own way of opening our life to God and discovering his presence within us.

I know there can be no full, mutual friendship between us,
    my God,
unless I have the desire to become conscious of you as a
    personal God.
The desire for this consciousness is your gift,
a sign that you are already touching my life.
Your interest in me is what should be most real in my life.
What else can compare to this?
May your Spirit awaken a sense of eagerness and love
    within me,
for without your Spirit,
I will simply remain asleep to the love that you continually
    pour into my life.

Examine your ideas about God. Think about the kind of relationship you have with God. Do you really believe that God has a personal interest in you? How does this belief affect your life? What form of prayer is the most suitable for awakening within you a deeper sense of God's presence?

A faithful commitment to one's religious tradition is a powerful force in the deepening of consciousness.

The primary purpose of all of the major religions is the deepening of consciousness. In their finer moments, the major religions intend to point the way to an experience of transcendence, to an experienced union with all that there is. First comes the experience which the founder awakens within his disciples, and then the experience is written down as a record and as a guide for future generations. From the writings, a logical ordering of beliefs and rules comes into being. Sometimes the emphasis on the writings overshadows the reason why they exist, but they are not ends in themselves. The writings are meant to lead back to the original experience which gave them birth. They are meant to be aids for the development of a loving consciousness, a communion with the transcendent, a communion with all of life.

One of the greatest joys a faithful commitment to one's religious tradition can offer is the opportunity to be a part of a community that shares the experience of faith and deeper consciousness. A loving and believing community is a powerful support for the growth of a unifying consciousness that embraces God and his creation, an embrace that brings us wholeness and joy. This is what we were created to experience, and it is this to which religion is meant to lead us. If we are a part of a community which believes in this vision of life, then we have a powerful help that accompanies us on our own journey toward becoming more fully alive. Such a community will minister not only to our spiritual needs, but also to our physical ones. It will be a community of service and love, bound by a common loving consciousness from which the service springs. God will be present to such a community, giving it the strength to be what it is meant to be. For Christians, Jesus expressed this truth when he said, "For where two or three come together in my name, I am there with them" (Matthew 18:20).

Communities can become lopsided either by forgetting that religion is meant to lead to consciousness, or by forgetting that it is meant to lead to service. In our time, the former is the greater danger. Religion must be more than social service or else it misses its mark. Without prayer, meditation, and the quiet mind that leads to a deeper loving consciousness, there can still be service, but it loses its soul. Deep love must always be fed by contemplative awareness. Isn't there a parallel in our relationships with those we love? We want more than service from those who love us. We also want their presence with us, a presence that is born from a conscious awareness of love and communion.

Religion tells us about love in this life, but also about love in the next. It tells us that we are loved without end, that there is no time limit to God's caring for us, because we are destined to live beyond time. Religion gives us meaning in this life and meaning in the next, when our consciousness will be full. It tells us that our fullness is in God, and that without God there is nothing at all. The more conscious we become of this, the more we experience what is real.

Sometimes our journey of consciousness takes us to

the consideration of other religions. We learn from them what we can without having to leave our own religious tradition. For some people, this kind of openness to other religions enriches their understanding of their own traditions. This need never mean that all religions are the same. One remains in one's own religious tradition which is regarded as the cradle of one's truth, while at the same time learning from the way in which God speaks to others. Whatever leads to true consciousness can be accepted. Whatever contradicts one's own tradition can be avoided.

All of the major religions have their own ways of leading their adherents to deeper consciousness. For many in the Christian tradition, the Bible and the sacraments are the guides that point to the deeper realities often overlooked in daily life. They are the signs and the reality of Christ's presence to the community which cherishes them. If we believe this, then the celebration of the eucharist (the Lord's Supper) becomes a celebration of Christ's presence among us. But at the same time, it makes us aware of something else that is always and everywhere true—that Christ is present always and everywhere in our lives. The celebration commemorates the death and resurrection of Christ, reminding us that what happened to Christ will also happen to us. In fact, if we are serious about our journey into deeper consciousness, what happened to Christ is already happening to us. Every day we are called to die to selfishness and rise to love. Religion is meant to make us conscious of this imperative. So it is with every sacrament. Each sacrament leads us into a deeper state of conscious awareness of our relationship with God.

For Christians, Jesus Christ is the ultimate sacrament of the presence of God. Jesus incarnates what was always true—that God was always present among us, loving us. But human beings need to see the signs of love. Don't we seek these signs from those we love? "Show me," we say. And so God showed us by becoming incarnate, helping us to become more conscious of the love and commitment he always has toward us. Knowing the life of Christ and meditating on his word, we come to understand that he is one with us, and that we are one with each other.

At times, we may have had experiences within our own religious traditions that did not seem life-giving to us. Churches and religious groups are made up of human beings. We have to accept their imperfections as God accepts ours. It is important not to pull away from our faith community because it is imperfect. We must try to recapture the core experience that caused the community to form in the first place. That core experience was the vital experience of God's love and presence revealed in time, a presence which invited all people to become one in love. That, of course, is what consciousness, at its deepest level, is all about. If we discover that in our own tradition, then our original religious faith will become a gateway to consciousness. It will offer an indispensable experience that will help us to become more fully awake.

I ask your pardon, my God,
because at times I have undervalued the treasure in my
    own religious tradition
and missed the revelation you wanted to share with me.
At times, I have judged my religious tradition harshly,
    perhaps unfairly.
What makes this so embarrassing is that I've probably
    misunderstood many of its teachings,
failing to see how you were trying to communicate with
    me within its midst.

I want to appreciate more deeply my religious community
   that shares its faith and fellowship with me,
helping me to grow in my awareness of you.
And I want to appreciate more deeply those communities
   that follow religious traditions other than my own.
May I be open to what they can say to me
and respect their sincerity as they search for you.

In what ways does your religious tradition deepen your consciousness of God's presence in your life? In what ways does it deepen the sense of communion with others? Have you sometimes missed the essential significance of what your religious tradition tries to convey because its members did not live up to your expectations?

There is no successful journey toward consciousness without expectations, but the wrong expectations can derail the journey.

It is beneficial to have some expectations about our journey toward consciousness. We can expect that the journey will lead toward wholeness and joy, toward a life-giving communion with God, toward a oneness with our brothers and sisters. Without these expectations, we most likely would not undertake the journey at all. But it wouldn't necessarily be beneficial to have our hearts set on particular expectations. If we did that, we might be disappointed.

There is a charming story about a girl who wanted a bicycle for Christmas. The girl's mother seemed to hint that she might get it. At least, that is how the girl interpreted what her mother said. To make the evidence even

more compelling, an unusually large cardboard box appeared in a corner of the basement a few days before
Christmas. There were no markings on the box, but the box
was about the size of a bicycle. On Christmas morning, the
girl's mother invited her to open the box. The girl reached
in expectantly, but then her face changed to an expression
of puzzlement. What was this thing, she wondered. As she
pulled out the contents of the box, she found herself staring at a mattress.

"You complained about how lumpy your old mattress
was," her mother said. "I wanted you to have something
comfortable to sleep on. I hope you'll sleep better now.
Merry Christmas, honey."

I read this story many years ago somewhere, and never
forgot it because it seems like a paradigm of life. Many
times life seems not to give us what we want, but perhaps
what we finally get is what is best. Our particular expectations are often unfulfilled, and so it seems wise not to be
too attached to them. If we are people of faith, our general
expectation will be that God will give us what is best for
our lives, given the circumstances in which we live. I think
this might well apply to our expectations about consciousness, for what is life but consciousness?

We should not expect that the journey toward fuller
consciousness will always be marked with peace and joy.
They will be there, of course. The more we relegate our
egos to their proper place, the more we will experience
peace and joy in this life. The fullness of peace and joy,
however, are only in the resurrected life, where no sorrow
or pain of any kind will be able to touch us.

> And I saw the Holy City, the new Jerusalem, coming
> down out of heaven from God, prepared and ready, like
> a bride dressed to meet her husband. I heard a loud
> voice speaking from the throne: "Now God's home is
> with [humankind]! He will live with them, and they

shall be his people. God himself will be with them, and
he will be their God. He will wipe away all tears from
their eyes. There will be no more death, no more grief
or crying, or pain. The old things have disappeared"
(Revelation 21:2-4).

People of faith have the expectation that this experience
will be theirs. They believe that something of this experience will touch them even in this life. Wise believers,
however, will also be prepared for the experience of suffering as a part of their journey toward consciousness. The
more conscious a person becomes, the more he or she
becomes aware of personal faults and failings. The darker
side of the unconscious comes into awareness. Repressed
feelings and unresolved conflicts will have to be dealt
with. As a person's consciousness expands, these elements
float to the surface and break into his or her awareness.
The necessity of dealing with these elements may not be a
part of one's original expectations, but facing up to them
will be a necessary part of the journey.

Growth in consciousness presupposes a kind of death,
a reality that sometimes escapes our expectations. We
must die to selfishness, mixed-up priorities, and all the
illusions that hinder our growth in awareness. The
hindrances that need to die are buried deep within us.
Only gradually do we become more aware of them, and
their death is often painful to us. We should not be
surprised, then, that the journey toward consciousness is
accompanied by suffering. The faster we let go of self-
centeredness, the more quickly we pass through the suffering that comes from hanging on to ourselves. This is a
part of the journey through which we must pass. In the
darkness, it may even seem sometimes that God is absent,
and we may wonder if the journey is worth the effort. It is
only when we experience the deepening presence of God

and some of the joys of fuller consciousness that we discover that the joys are worth the price.

> When a woman is about to give birth, she is sad because her hour of suffering has come; but when the baby is born, she forgets her suffering, because she is happy that a baby has been born into the world. That is how it is with you: now you are sad, but I will see you again, and your hearts will be filled with gladness, the kind of gladness that no one can take away from you (John 16:21-22).

So it is with us as we grow in our experience of unity with God, with one another, and with the entire universe. Our expectation is that, in the end, our journey toward consciousness will turn out all right.

The journey toward consciousness unfolds differently in each one of us. We become awake at different times, each one according to his or her own rhythm. We become conscious in different ways and in different degrees, each one according to his or her own personality. It makes sense, then, to begin the journey without particular and detailed expectations. We cannot know exactly how our own paths will unfold. We only know that the journey is accompanied by both joy and suffering. But when it reaches its fulfillment in the resurrection, there will be only joy.

I journey toward you, my God,
with the expectation that you are good,
and that life is good because it flows from you.
I travel in some darkness, my God,
because I don't know all the twists and turns of the
    journey.

It's best that I not worry about that,
because you are in charge of where I am going.
So I'm trying to let go of expectations about how long the
   journey should be,
or what particular directions it should take.
I will have faith in you even if the journey leads to
   suffering.
It's enough for me to know that you are trustworthy,
and that I am becoming whole in oneness with you.
For this, I am grateful.
You are the gateway to consciousness.
In loving you, I will find myself,
my brothers and sisters,
and the wholeness to which you have called me.
Those are my expectations.

What are your expectations as you journey on your way
to a deeper awareness of God? What do you hope for in
your search for union with your relatives and friends? Has
your growth in awareness ever been compromised by
false or unreal expectations? Are some of those false or
unreal expectations still with you now? Only a rigorous
and honest self-evaluation can reveal that to you and set
you free from the poison of unreasonable hopes.

The journey toward consciousness can be completed only with the acceptance of suffering.

In his life on earth Jesus made his prayers and requests
with loud cries and tears to God, who could save him
from death. Because he was humble and devoted, God

heard him. But even though he was God's Son, he
learned through his sufferings to be obedient. When he
was made perfect, he became the source of eternal
salvation for all who obey him (Hebrews 5:7-9).

It seems strange to think of suffering as a gateway to
consciousness, but suffering is inescapable, and we have
to learn something from it before we can be made whole.
The message of the Bible is that Jesus was called by the
Father to accept his suffering and death, and that his
loving acceptance brought him resurrected life. Suffering
and death taught his human nature obedience to the law
of life—that we must die in order to rise. How else can we
find our own wholeness except through this obedience?
Through his acceptance of death, Jesus was given a new
life, and in his resurrection, we find the hope of our own.

The acceptance of what cannot be changed is part of the
obedience to which we are called. The struggle to accept
what cannot be changed involves the letting go of the ego
which naturally fights to keep itself in charge of things.
The struggle is perceived as a suffering, which of course it
is. But the suffering is diminished when we put the ego to
rest and finally accept those things in our lives that cannot
be changed. Our refusal to accept reality may be what
causes us the most suffering. When our energies are
soaked up by the prolonged struggle, our abilities to be
aware of other aspects of life are diminished.

Suffering often teaches us that some attitude we have
about our lives is causing us harm. A woman who generally enjoyed good health started to experience severe
stomach pains. She confided in a friend, saying that not
only was her health deteriorating, but that she was no
longer able to pray. Her peaceful awareness of God had
disappeared.

Her friend responded by asking, "Mary, do you think
you might be angry at God because of the death of your

child?" Mary found it impossible at first to consider her friend's suggestion, because anger toward God was a terrible thing in her eyes. She could never admit that she felt anger toward God. But as time went on, it became quite clear to her that this was the problem. Her attitude toward God was causing the suffering. When she was able to admit her feelings toward God, deal with them and accept reality, the suffering subsided.

It was Mary's suffering, her stomach pains, and her inability to pray that finally revealed her deeper problem. Sometimes suffering tells us that there is an attitude within ourselves that needs to change. The suffering calls us to deal with an obstacle that is keeping us from being fully alive. Perhaps many of us have perceived this phenomenon in our own lives. It is simply a part of the human condition. If we catch the meaning of this kind of suffering and learn from it, we regain our ability to grow more conscious of God's love and the goodness of life. If we run away from this kind of suffering without consider-ing its meaning, we suffer without knowing why and without much chance of being healed. Missing the mes-sage, we miss our chance for wholeness.

The experience of suffering can expand our conscious-ness in yet another way. Suffering can teach compassion for others, and in our compassion, we discover that we are all one. Perhaps for this to happen, we need not only a sensitive heart and a deep experience of faith, but also a deep awareness of the sufferings that other people have to endure.

There is a beautiful story about a young woman who brought her dead baby to the Buddha. She asked the Buddha to restore her baby's life. The Buddha replied that first she must go to every house in her village and ask if there were any people in the house who had never heard of death, or who had not experienced the death of someone they knew. If she were to find such people, she was to ask them for a grain of rice. The young woman went to every house and asked the question, but she could find no one who had not been touched by someone's death. At the end of the day, she had collected not one grain of rice. But the experience taught her compassion, a feeling of solidarity with others in their suffering.

Suffering is an inevitable part of life for each of us. When we cannot remove suffering from someone's life, we need to sit quietly with the person, offering our love and support. In the experience of compassion, we become more alive to our interconnectedness with one another. We share similar life experiences, and in this, we find a oneness which gives birth to love. Perhaps this could never happen without the experience of suffering. In this sense too, suffering serves to expand our conscious awareness and our love for others.

To be a disciple of Jesus, one has to learn the meaning of suffering. We are called to remove the sufferings that are removable, and this is a choice for life. We are called to accept the sufferings that cannot be removed, and this too is a choice for life. The results of this choice are wisdom, compassion, and birth into greater consciousness, which finally culminates in the resurrected life.

You know how much I abhor suffering, my God,
and how much I try to escape it.
Help me to see which sufferings I cause unnecessarily
both to myself and to others.
May I learn something from the unavoidable sufferings of
    my life,
and may I learn compassion for others in their sufferings
    and difficulties.

For all the sufferings which have taught me something I
needed to learn, I give thanks.
For all the sufferings that have enabled me to be
compassionate, I give thanks.
Each time I have learned from my sufferings, I have been
brought to new life.
This is how you touch me with your miracles, my God.
You find what is sick and dying in me,
and you change it into new life.
Increase my faith in you,
so that through your healing touch,
everything within me may be an occasion for growth
toward wholeness.

Sometimes suffering teaches us that we are infected by
faulty attitudes that set us in opposition to God, to life.
Have you experienced this kind of suffering in your life?
How have you allowed it to lead you back to wholeness?
Does the experience of your own suffering lead you to an
active compassion for others? Are you able to be grateful
for the lessons that suffering has taught you?

*Without gratitude for the gifts of life, we can-
not be fully awake to what we have received.*

When Jesus cured the ten lepers, only one, a Samaritan,
came back to give thanks. Jesus responded by saying:

> "There were ten men who were healed. Where are the
> other nine? Why is this foreigner the only one who came
> back to give thanks to God?" And Jesus said to him,
> "Get up and go; your faith has made you well" (Luke
> 17:17-19).

Gratitude makes us appreciate more deeply the gifts that are a part of our lives. We have received very much from God and from the people who love us. Gratitude forges bonds between the one who gives and the one who receives. We become more fully awake when we are thankful for life and its gifts.

An incident in my own life taught me to be grateful for those who love me, and more awake to the beauty of their gifts. About three times a year, friends of mine in a nearby city invite me for a lavish dinner. They prepare homemade bread and a tantalizing array of hors d'oeuvres. On one occasion, they put tiger lily petals in the gravy that garnished a prime cut of beef. On another occasion they served fish prepared from a medieval recipe. After dinner one evening, my friend Jim said, "You know, this is how Eileen shows her love for you." I had never really thought about that, but that awareness deepened my appreciation of the menu. That awareness also deepened my relationship with these two friends. Before I more fully understood the love, I was eating only half-consciously.

My experience illustrates something about the story of the leper who returned to give thanks. He understood the meaning of gratitude, the necessity of appreciating a favor received, the importance of seeing the love with which a favor is given. If we do not appreciate that everything about our lives is a gift, we live only half-consciously. There may be something we can learn from the leper who came back to give thanks. What should we be thankful for in our lives?

Do we ever give thanks for our gifts and talents? Our native talents may have made us successful in life, but these talents are gifts. We have developed them, of course, but even the power to do that came from God. God constantly sustains our lives. If God were to cease being conscious of us, we would not be. We exist only because we are remembered by God. We act only because we are empowered by God. That is why Jesus said we could do nothing without him. If we think otherwise, we miss the truth about ourselves.

What is it in our lives that is not a gift? When we recognize our gifts and give thanks, we become aware of God the giver. The leper who returned to give thanks was more lovingly aware of Jesus than the other nine. Whenever we are genuinely grateful to people, we have a deeper sense of their presence, a deeper sense of their connection with us. This is simply an ordinary experience of life for those who are awake. We can have this same experience with God. When we do, we become more aware of what our relationship to God is. We become more aware of how much we are loved.

Do we ever give thanks for our friends? Our friends are God's gifts to us. Now we might think that it is because of our irresistible charm that we have people in our lives who love us. But if God had not created them and put them into our lives, how could they be present to us? As to our charm—well to the extent that we have any—that too is a native disposition placed in us by God. If we bring any joy to others, we have God to thank for that.

Pray for the gift of becoming more deeply grateful. The leper who returned to give thanks was certainly more alive than the ones who did not. He had a clearer understanding of the One who healed him. Being aware that he had been touched by someone who loved him, that alone would have made him more joyful than the other nine who were not as fully conscious. What about us? Would there be more joy in our lives if we were more truly grateful?

Our task in life should be to become more conscious, more aware that everything within us and around us is a loving gift of God. The more clearly we understand that, the more deeply we know we are loved. And that brings joy. We never come to know that kind of joy, however, unless we prayerfully think about what it means to be grateful.

You are a lover of truth, my God,
and so you are a lover of gratitude.
Gratitude is truth,
and I need the inspiration of your Spirit to remember this.
May my prayer be one of thanksgiving to you,
for everything I have is the result of your goodness to me.
Everything I am able to be for others
comes from the gift of your Spirit
which enables me to radiate your goodness.

Who or what do you take for granted in your life? Choose one person or one thing that you take for granted, and instead, be grateful to the giver. Realize what you have been given so that you might become more aware of the love which is constantly a part of your life.

When we become fully awake, the signs will be there for everyone to read.

The fully awake person is a person who has put on the mind of Christ, a person who is conscious of life's goodness. Such a person can be recognized by the way she lives.

The person who is fully and lovingly conscious is one who lives by the Spirit. St. Paul tells us what this Spirit does and how we might recognize his presence: "But the

Spirit produces love, joy, peace, patience, kindness, goodness, faithfulness, humility, and self-control" (Galatians
5:22-23). If these signs exist in our lives, we know that we
are becoming awake, and that we are being transformed
into the consciousness of Christ. Jesus said, "A healthy tree
bears good fruit, but a poor tree bears bad fruit" (Matthew
7:17). We can know whether or not we are on the right path
by the fruit we bear, and others will know this about us,
too. A loving consciousness and the actions that flow from
it are the fruits of the Spirit. The Spirit changes us, simply
because love changes us, and the change becomes obvious
to all who are a part of our lives.

There is a charming story about a group of people in a
retirement home whose lives were changed when they
were allowed to have a pet in their rooms. Having something to love gave them a new purpose. The giving and
receiving of affection sparked a renewed interest in life,
and the resulting transformation became noticeable to
those who knew them. One might suppose, of course, that
a shared human love would bring even more beneficial
results. And what can we say when it is a question of
divine love?

The gifts of the Spirit are already within us, at least as
potentials that can come to birth whenever we accept
them. We do not have to look for these gifts of the Spirit
outside of ourselves. We may miss this truth because the
Spirit's presence within us is often clouded over, so to
speak, by the egoism characteristic of those who have not
yet become awake. The journey toward consciousness
involves recognizing that the gifts of the Spirit are really
here, and that these gifts can bring us to a deeper experience of who we are meant to be. God is always present
within us, offering himself and his gifts which make us
whole. God's presence is so much a part of our lives that
we simply cannot escape from it.

> Where could I go to escape from you? Where could I get
> away from your presence? If I went up to heaven, you
> would be there; if I lay down in the world of the dead,
> you would be there. If I flew away beyond the east or
> lived in the farthest place in the west, you would be
> there to lead me, you would be there to help me (Psalm
> 139:7-10).

The joyful task of life is to become ever more deeply conscious of God's loving, compassionate presence, and to bear the fruits which result from that consciousness. In this way, we become a help to others in their own journey toward God.

The gifts of the Spirit truly transform us, and for that reason those who live according to the fruits of the Spirit already understand something of the resurrected life. They understand that, because of the fruits of the Spirit within them, the resurrected life has in some sense already begun. Experiencing the gifts of the Spirit, they discover a sense of wholeness and joy, and they become signs of life for others. We need to find the way to realize this experience for ourselves, to see that the promise of the Spirit's gifts applies personally to each one of us. Then not only will we ourselves be awake wherever we are, but we will also become signs to those whose lives we touch. As more of us become signs of life to one another, perhaps we will discover more deeply the meaning of Christian community. We will experience it as a community of shared loving consciousness made possible by the presence of the God who gives life to us all.

May I know the fruits of your Spirit in my life, my God,
so that I might be like you,
having your mind and becoming one with your life.

My journey into consciousness begins with you and ends
    with you.
I ask that in this journey I might realize my oneness not
    only with you,
but also with all of my brothers and sisters.
I ask that my life might be of value to them
and that we might become signs to one another
of the love that you put into each one of us.
May the experience of our oneness deepen within us in
    the present moment,
and reach its fullness in the ages to come.
May I overcome the obstacles within me
that keep this experience from coming into full bloom.

How does your life reflect the presence of the Spirit to
the family and community in which you live? What is it in
your life that is out of harmony with the "love, joy, peace,
patience, kindness, goodness, faithfulness, humility, and
self-control" which are the marks of God's Spirit? Can you
recognize the presence of the Spirit in those with whom
you live? What do they teach you about the possibility of
developing the potentials for love and wholeness that are
within yourself?

THREE

The Obstacles to a Fully Conscious Life

"Every day I try to be aware of the present moment, and every day my mind wanders away from it," the young man complained. "What can I do to stop the wandering?"

"Search for the obstacles that keep you from being fully present to where you are," the teacher answered. "Root them out and toss them away. Ask yourself what price you are willing to pay to be free."

> Jesus said, "If your hand or your foot makes you lose your faith, cut if off and throw it away! It is better for you to enter life without a hand or a foot than to keep both hands and both feet and be thrown into the eternal fire."
>
> —Matthew 18:8

If we want to become fully alive, we need to
remove the obstacles to our consciousness.

We are wonderful people, unconditionally loved by
God and made in his image. That is the truth. But if we
know ourselves well enough, we discover that we carry
flaws. That is the truth too. Our flaws keep us from being
fully conscious and fully free.

A Greek storyteller once wrote that when Achilles was
born, his mother dipped him into a mythical river which
gave his body protection from spears and arrows. A pretty
good deal since he was destined to wind up on the battle
field! But like most good deals, there was a flaw. His
mother had to hold him someplace when she dipped him
into the river. She chose to hold him by the heel. Later in
life when Achilles became a warrior, his enemies discovered the secret of his vulnerability. Guess where they
aimed their arrows!

No matter how wonderful we are, we all have our own
version of an Achilles heel, a flaw of some kind. The less
fortunate among us have more than one. God still loves us
of course, but our flaws keep us from experiencing his
love. Our flaws are obstacles to our consciousness of God's
presence. Imagine a situation in which someone loved
you, but anger, independence, or indifference kept you
from experiencing that love. Don't we all have some
familiarity with this kind of situation? Our flaws keep us
from responding fully to someone who loves us. Perhaps
the flaws of our loved ones prevent them from responding
fully to us. That is how we are sometimes with God.

Our flaws are obstacles to a full and loving consciousness, and for that reason, we need to know what our
obstacles are. How else can we deal with them and remove
their deadening effects?

The part of us where our flaws make their home can be

called our shadow. If we are to become whole, we need to be honest and get in touch with the shadow side of our lives. The shadow is what keeps us from the light of a fuller loving consciousness, our birthright from God. Honest introspection is the only way we can get in touch with our shadow and finally overcome its power. Periodically we need to do some unflinching self-examination. Alcoholics Anonymous recognizes this need by insisting that recovering alcoholics make a "fearless moral inventory." Catholics have the sacrament of reconciliation, which is meant to accomplish a similar need. But flaws die hard and new ones can always rise to take the place of those that we seem to have vanquished. For those who truly want to grow in a loving consciousness, honest self-evaluation is a process that should be as much a part of life as breathing and eating.

When life seems to be going sour, it makes sense to look for the cause. If we experience a discontent with life that seems to have no explanation or reason, that could be a sign of the presence of obstacles in our lives. Often enough, at least part of the cause might well be within. "Be alert, be on watch! Your enemy, the Devil, roams around like a roaring lion, looking for someone to devour" (1 Peter 5:8), scripture says. The unacknowledged shadow side of our personalities roams around within us, presenting obstacles to our ability to become fully conscious. The shadow side, which includes greed, envy, lust, and other personality defects, keeps us in darkness because it keeps us from love and communion with others. When we uncover the negative contents of our shadow side and deal with them, then we become free from being locked up within ourselves.

I know that I have flaws, my God,
although at times I may be somewhat unconscious
    of them.

I know it is your will that I should be set free
from the flaws that restrict my love.
It is only in this freedom that I'll be able to experience the
    full life
that you have destined for me to enjoy.
I ask for your light.
May I have the courage and honesty
to look at myself in the face of your presence within me.
Why should I try to hide my flaws from you, my God?
You already know them better than I do.
When I try to hide them, I only hide them from myself.
And it is when they are hidden that they do the most
    mischief.
Show me the obstacles that keep me from sensing your
love and presence, my God.

When you examine your life for your predominant
flaw, what do you find? What is your most harmful be-
havior? Greed? Lack of respect for others? Wasting your
time on trivialities? How does this misuse of your energy
keep you from tuning into a deeper awareness of life's
goodness?

*Without forgiving ourselves for our
flaws and failures, we are not free to
become fully conscious.*

Developing a deeper sense of awareness is a life-giving
goal, but when we think about it, it presents problems.
People who grow in sensitivity to the events of their lives
often become more aware not only of life's joys, but also

of life's frustrations and failures. Although most of us would prefer to suppress our awareness of our frustrations and failures, the effort involved in doing so dulls our consciousness. Too much energy is used in the process, energy that could be used for more positive experiences of consciousness. It is important that we admit our frustrations and failures to ourselves and accept them for what they are, forgiving ourselves in the process.

A middle-aged man had thrown away a college scholarship in his youth and wasted his early life on drugs. Although he recovered from the drug habit, his life was continually marked with regret for what he had thrown away. Squandering his educational opportunity was a tragedy, of course, but the greater tragedy was the bitter regret and self-recrimination with which he lived his life. These attitudes sapped his energy, making it more difficult for him to direct his thinking in more positive directions. He never learned to forgive himself.

Frustrations, mistakes, and failures are an inevitable part of every life. They show themselves in many different forms. A person whom you love very deeply doesn't love you. If only you were more loveable. You invest great personal energy in an important plan and it doesn't turn out. If only you had tried harder. You want something very much, but you don't get it. If only you were more successful. Life doesn't give you what you want when you want it. If only you were more worthy. And if all this is not enough, then add in your awareness of all of your limitations and mistakes.

Often, though, our view of ourselves is skewed. How important it is for us to see our lives more realistically, and to forgive ourselves for our mistakes and failures, both real and imagined. We need to see our positive side along with the negative. We need to do the same for others.

We have to acknowledge life's unpleasantries. If we

don't consciously deal with them, they will deal with us. We must forgive ourselves and put our mistakes to rest. Otherwise we will never be free enough to turn ourselves to the more positive aspects of life. The whole tenor of our lives depends on what we do with our consciousness, where we direct our awareness. We have some control over our moods and the quality of our psychological life. A lot depends on our willingness to let go of our failures and to be more awake to the joys that surround us. For many of us, that's an ability that rarely comes into full bloom.

The power that we have for self-fulfillment or self-destruction may seem frightening. There are times in our lives when the power can be used decisively either way. That is why it pays to be more aware of which way we are going. Introspection helps, but then so does faith in the light that God puts within us. We know that God accompanies us on our life journey, enabling us to forgive ourselves as he forgives us. God is closer to us than our own heartbeat, and his strength is ours whenever we wish to accept it. Nothing can ultimately go wrong for us if we are determined to remain in God's hands and to be open to the direction of his Spirit which offers us a new way to live.

There are parts of my life that I carry as a burden, my God.
Foolish actions that have harmed both others and myself,
disappointment with others and with myself,
a lack of fulfillment that I could have avoided.
All of these are a part of my life that I present to you.
May I learn something from all of these unpleasant
    situations
through the courage to face myself as I am,
with the forgiveness that comes from you.

As I acknowledge the frustrations and failures in my
    own life,
I will not be afraid,
for you always love and accept me as I am.
I believe this, my God,
and I believe that your strength is with me
as I journey through the course of my life.
Relying on your love,
I can grow in my ability to trust and to forgive myself.

Are there some actions or attitudes in your life for which
you have not forgiven yourself? How does lack of forgiveness destroy quietness of mind and sap your energy for
more positive living? Have you forgiven others who might
have hurt you?

The greatest obstacle to a loving consciousness is a noisy mind.

There are different kinds of noisy minds. An immoral
mind will be a noisy mind, because it is filled with the
clatter of its own ego. It loses itself in its passions. But even
a virtuous mind can be a noisy mind if it loses its center.
Such a mind is filled with noise because it is pulled and
tugged by everything around it. It lacks depth of consciousness because its energies are scattered over a multi-
tude of concerns. Perhaps we have all had an experience
of this at some time. We find ourselves trying to juggle
three things at once, and somehow, in the midst of all this,
our mind flashes to things we have to do three hours in
the future. At the very least, we can make a decision to live

in the present moment and try to focus our scattered attention.

Sometimes, when we are lucky, we can withdraw from the confusion and take time to quiet our mind on a deeper level. Perhaps we can listen calmly to some music, look out of the window, or just relax quietly in a chair. If we can do this long enough, we become calm. We become centered, peaceful. And if there are any plans or decisions that must be made, we are in a good position to make them. When the mind is quiet, things become clearer. We become aware of what it is we need to do.

The greatest obstacle to the awareness of our present moment, our Achilles heel that prevents us from being more fully alive, is our noisy minds. Our minds are everywhere at once, and we have lost the art of knowing how to be where we are. That is the big flaw of our culture.

There is a humorous story about a statistician taking a drive in the country with his friend. His friend gives him a challenge: "Let's see how good you are at counting things. In a few moments we'll be passing my farm and the cows should be grazing in the north pasture. When we go by, tell me how many cows are in the field."

The car, travelling well beyond the speed limit, zoomed past the field in a matter of seconds.

"Well, did you see the cows?" the statistician's friend asked.

"Of course," replied the statistician nonchalantly.

"So how many did you count?"

"Forty seven."

"Why, that's right," replied the statistician's friend with amazement. "How on earth did you ever do that?"

"It's really very simple," he said. "I just counted the legs and divided by four."

In real life, of course, that would be impossible, but we live as if we believed such things could be done. We live our lives at top speed and clutter our minds with dozens of items. And in the process we lose our ability to sort them out and keep them in perspective. In real life, our statistician would have to slow down the car and simplify the counting procedure. So we too have to slow down to make sense of our lives.

Slowing down our minds so that they become more focused and less scattered is a prerequisite for being fully conscious and experiencing the presence of the God within and around us. It is within our power to do this. If we do not, we will not live our lives in the present moment. We'll be somewhere else.

When we get very good at quieting our minds, we'll be fully and calmly conscious even while living life on the run and doing all the active things we have to do. An Indian swami once said to me, "I am active, but my mind is always at rest." To get to that point, he spent time every day just quieting his mind. It is worth the time. A quiet mind serves us well and brings us pleasure not only in moments of meditation, but also in moments of activity. Perhaps though, we can only accept this when we actually experience the quietness within ourselves.

Help me to keep my life simple, my God.
You speak to the uncluttered mind,
and it hears you.
May I have such a mind.
May I have the insight and the strength
to root out of my life all the unnecessary noise
that causes me to lose sight of you and your gifts.

What creates the excessive noise in your mind? Could it be too much emphasis on competition, immoderate worry, excessive preoccupation with unnecessary activity, or a craving for things to be other than they are? Would your life be more pleasant if your mind were more quiet and peaceful?

The sources of many of our disturbances in life are the cravings that capture our minds.

Why are our minds so often disturbed? Isn't it usually because we crave something we cannot have and we refuse to let go of the craving?

A former patient of mine was told not to sit in front of his ex-wife's house after he was released from an alcoholism treatment center. His former wife no longer wanted a relationship with him, and every time he had gone to her house, he would leave and then get drunk. Unfortunately he did not follow the advice given to him. After leaving the center, he drove to where his wife lived and sat in front of her home. When he noticed another man in the house, he immediately sped off in anger, went into a tavern, and became heavily intoxicated. When he returned home, he drove into the garage, closed the door, and passed out. The car's engine was still running. The immediate cause of death was carbon monoxide poisoning, the underlying cause was alcoholism.

Or could we say, perhaps, that he died from craving someone he could not have, he died from an unquiet mind?

Are there any parallels—less fatal and extreme, of course—in your own life? What is there that you won't let go of? You have to know where you are stuck. Look at yourself. Is there a craving that disturbs or preoccupies you? Does it distort your consciousness?

In Luke 12:16-20, Jesus tells a parable about man who

had an abundance of crops. The man wondered what to do with them until finally he decided to pull down his barns and build bigger ones. That very night though, the man had to give up his life. What use were his goods to him then? In the parable, God called this man a fool.

His preoccupation with things he didn't even need distorted his perspective on who he was and what his life meant. God could have come at any time, not only to call him to eternal life, but to touch him with love in this life. But what if God's voice couldn't penetrate through all the noise and craving? How then could the man ever have become more conscious? A full, loving consciousness is the result of a response to who God is. But if the mind is not still, if it is unnecessarily preoccupied, it cannot respond in a meaningful way. Where are you preoccupied? Where are you caught? And does being preoccupied and being hooked make things any better for you? If not, why not decide to be free?

I want to live this day with attention, my God.
I want to become aware of my own cravings
so that I can defuse their harmful effects on my life.
Sometimes I'm not fully aware of my cravings,
but even then, their destructiveness touches me.
I know you have the power to make me free,
but you respect my wishes.
You give me nothing that I'm not willing to receive.
And yet you are always present to me
with the gentle motion of your love.
May I respond and be set free
from the cravings that rob me of my true life.

Can you identify with the man in the parable who was preoccupied about storing his excess crops? In what sense are your cravings destructive? Discover that, and you'll find the thieves that rob you of your freedom to be fully alive. Believe that you can become freer than you are.

Lack of belief in ourselves blocks our ability to grow in awareness.

A friend of mine was offered the position of head nurse in the hospital department where she had worked for six years. After some deliberation, she refused the position, fearing that she was not qualified. Her supervisor and peers thought differently, and urged her to reconsider. They were very much aware of her abilities as a nurse. They knew about her capacity for compassionate caring, as well as her capacity for leadership. Nothing they said to her, however, could induce her to change her mind. She refused the position.

Of course, the nurse was under no obligation to accept, but her reason for not accepting was unfortunate. She was motivated by a self-doubt that had no basis in fact. As a result, she allowed her unfounded doubt to rob her of an occasion for growth. She lost an opportunity to become more conscious of her own leadership potential.

Sometimes we don't pursue certain goals because we think they are unattainable. This is a problem that seems to have its effects even in the animal world. A behavioral psychologist once stocked an aquarium with two kinds of fish—predator fish and fish that they feed on. Both classes of fish were separated by a pane of clear glass. At first, the predators repeatedly swam into the glass in a vain attempt to grab a meal. After a time, though, they gave up. When the psychologist removed the pane of glass, the tranquility inside the aquarium continued. The reason? The predator fish continued to believe that catching a meal was an impossible task.

We can become conditioned to failure. Those who succeed in life are the ones who refuse to be conditioned. This is crucial. Many times a person's journey into deeper consciousness is aborted by failure. What an unfortunate tragedy! In reality, our attempts to grow in consciousness are fraught with failures. We try to learn how to stay awake, how to be aware of life's joys, how to learn from life's sorrows, how to be aware of God's presence. And we keep forgetting.

Can you remember when you first learned how to ride a bicycle? Did you fall off very often? It took me months to learn how to keep from falling. For some of us, things like this take time! So it is with many other things in life. So it is with learning how to be awake, learning how to be where we are, learning how to pray, learning how to be aware of God and how to let that awareness grow into the service of others. When we fail or forget, then we begin again. People who do that finally learn what it is like to be fully alive.

There are different ways to look at our failures. If we believe deeply enough in life and in God, a failure in one area may open up an opportunity somewhere else. Reflect on your life to see whether or not this is true. Sometimes we can use our failures and turn them into successes. A young woman once told her spiritual director that she was unable to pray. Every time she tried to pray, she kept hearing her favorite tunes playing in her head! Since she did not know how to control these unwanted musical interruptions, she considered her prayer life to be a failure. Finally, she thought about giving up prayer all together. After some time, her spiritual director found a solution. Instead of fighting her musical distractions, the woman was encouraged to take the tunes and put her own words to them, thus making them a prayer. Quite a creative solution to what initially seemed to be a failure!

For those who believe in God and in themselves, failures need not signify the end of anything. Instead, they can signify new opportunities to try again in new ways.

May I learn to believe more deeply in myself, my God,
and in your power at work within me.
I want to be more conscious of your presence
and of the way you work in my life,
but often I forget to stay awake.
May my repeated failures not discourage me.
Help me to see the opportunities that might be buried
    within them.
If I ever give up on trying to live my life fully,
I will betray your gift and lose my chance for joy.
Preserve me, my God, from that kind of infidelity.

What challenges do you avoid because of fear of failure? What have you forfeited in life through lack of perseverance? Has lack of perseverance derailed your journey toward intimacy with God, and has a lack of creativity kept you from living a more fully conscious life?

If we can't get in through the door, we'll have to go in by another way.

If the door is blocked and you can't see any other way in, you're in trouble. But then again, maybe not. How creative are you in working around the blocks that darken the reality of God's presence in your life?

In Luke 5:17-20 the story is told about some friends of a paralyzed man who creatively solve a problem. They try to take the paralyzed man to Jesus, but discover that they can't get into the house where Jesus is staying because of the crowd blocking the door. Instead of giving up and going home, they find an ingenious solution. They remove part of the roof and lower the man into the middle of a group of people in front of Jesus. They are rewarded for their ingenuity. The paralyzed man is healed.

The healing, of course, was God's gift, but no more so than the creativity of overcoming the block that kept the paralytic from Jesus in the first place. The ingenuity of the paralytic's friends was the first step in making the healing possible. Creative insights are among God's greatest gifts because they enable us to remove our blocks to freedom and wholeness. We become awake to this possibility when we try to identify our own blocks to wholeness and search for creative ways either to remove them or to work around them.

For this to be successful in our lives, we have to be honest in our searching. A man in a hospital concluded that his illness was caused, in part, by his long and deep seated hatred for his brother. The hatred had developed after an intense fight many years ago, but it remained buried in his heart long after the fight was over. Since he no longer knew where his brother was, he saw that he'd have to make peace without being able to ask for reconciliation and forgiveness. His solution? He decided to pray for his brother. And the fruits of this prayer finally brought him the peace and wholeness for which he had been searching. Here is a creative solution to a particular obstacle that is open to anyone who thinks about it. The problem, perhaps, is that not too many people do.

The more awake we are to creative solutions for problems that seem to have no obvious answers, the more attentive we'll be to God's inspiration within ourselves. God's inspiration is always creative, and oftentimes, our experience of pain nourishes the creative process. When we hurt enough, we're more likely to find a way around the obstacles that block the solution to our problems. The paralytic probably wouldn't have gone through the hole in the roof to find Jesus if he had merely been suffering from a small cut in his finger. The man in the hospital might not have prayed intensely for his brother had it not been for his own deep need for reconciliation. Suffering can be a great motivator, if we don't cover it up with frenetic activity or deadening distractions.

Perhaps what makes us most open to the possibility of creative solutions is a quiet mind. The creative solutions to obstacles are often already within us. It's the quiet that allows them to come into consciousness. A quiet mind can listen to what is best within itself. It can hear the advice of friends, but above all, it can hear the Spirit of God who communicates more clearly in stillness. Creative insights sometimes come in the midst of daily activity, but when that happens, it's usually because their seeds were sown in stillness.

Honesty in admitting the obstacles to our wholeness, and the ability to read what our sufferings tell us about our blocks, plus a quiet mind that allows inventive solutions to arise—these are the avenues through which God's creative spirit enters into us. They are our ways of cooperating with the God who offers us the power and the insight to cope with the obstacles of our lives. Spiritual healing is God's will for us. To be awake is to discover how to receive it.

Nature itself employs creative solutions to overcome the obstacles that thwart its goals. To enable the giraffe to widen its opportunities for feeding, nature gave it a long neck. To protect certain insects from their predators, nature gave them the ability to blend with their sur-roundings. To shield the turtle from its swifter enemies, nature gave it a hard shell. Isn't God at work in all of this? And God is at work in us, giving us a gift that we alone possess, the gift of conscious ingenuity. Was it given, in part, so that we could creatively overcome the obstacles to loving and being fully alive?

It is in human beings that God finds conscious partners in his creative activities. We have been given a share in what God himself does. Perhaps in those moments when we use our creative energies to circumvent the obstacles around the door, we imitate what God is always doing. For God constantly finds ways to circumvent the obstacles around the door to our hearts.

"The Lord says, 'Let my people return to me. Remove every obstacle from their path! Build the road and make it ready!'" (Isaiah 57:14).

May I be conscious of what blocks my path to you,
    my God,
and creative in opening my heart to your presence.
So much of my life is complicated by obstacles of my own
    making.
It is in becoming free of them that I discover the saving
    power of your presence in my life.
Without such a liberation, how could I ever be more
    deeply aware of you?
I pray for an increased faith in your creative power
    working in my life.
In listening to you, may I find a way out of my problems
that otherwise might keep me locked up within myself.

Think of a problem in your life where you seem stuck, where all the doors to a solution seem closed. Calm your mind and ask the creative power of Christ's Spirit to enlighten you. Come into the presence of Christ and pray about the problem. This may take time, and the solution may not simply be the removal of the problem, but may involve a changed attitude that will enable you to live with it. Let go of any particular expectations. Simply accept what comes as you open yourself to the creative power of God's Spirit within you.

Get hold of yourself. Let go.

Our fears rob us of being fully alive to God's presence within ourselves and in the world around us. And it is often fear that siphons away our creative energy to remove the blocks that prevent us from being fully conscious. Unreasonable fear is a terrible enemy. And so Jesus tells us to get hold of ourselves, and let go.

Get hold of ourselves and let go? Is there a paradox here? How can one do both? When the apostles saw Jesus walking toward them over a turbulently foaming sea, they thought he was a ghost and cried out in alarm. Seeing their fear, Jesus told them to take courage and to put fear aside (see Mark 6:50). In other versions of this story, Jesus tells them to get hold of themselves. The meaning, of course, is the same. But while getting hold of themselves, they are to let go of their fear. He seems to be telling them to be in control, and at the same time to let go. A neat trick if one can do it. How can that be done?

The problem is that many of us try to be in total control of our lives, and we discover that the results are disastrous. We can't handle things merely by trying to be in control, and that is what's behind the famous AA saying, "Let go and let God." But perhaps there are two different kinds of control. We can be in control by trying to run our lives by ourselves, or we can be in control by taking our lives and handing them over to God with faith and trust. What we control is our free decision in faith to give our lives to God, and to cooperate with the Spirit of God as he leads and guides us on our life journey. But that kind of control is also a letting go. It is a relinquishing of our concerns into the hands of God so that we can live our lives without energy-depleting fear.

When the apostles got hold of themselves and let go of their fear, the winds were calmed and they were able to navigate their boat without being threatened by the storm. What if they had not trusted Jesus and instead had made the decision not to let go of their fear? One can only guess. The storm would not have abated, and the apostles would have been left to deal with the wind and the waves on their own. And had the situation dragged on, the whole experience would have been far worse than it was. Can we learn something from this?

God wants to preserve us from many of the problems and unpleasant situations that come when we try to do things completely on our own. There are no promises that storms won't be a part of our lives, but there is a promise that we won't have to navigate through them by ourselves. The apostles experienced the storm. But they also experienced the power of God which led them safely through it. God was able to come to them with effective power when they let go of their fear.

No one can be fully awake to the best and deepest parts of life without getting hold of oneself and letting go. Take a major concern of your life that tends to dominate your thoughts and your feelings. If you carry this concern without knowing how to let go, your consciousness gets stuck. If too much of your energy is absorbed in the concern, you can't be awake to what is going on in the rest

of your life. In fact, you can become so bogged down with
a problem that you lose your creative energy to find your
way out of it. By trying to be too much in control, you may
become less conscious of the potential experiences that
make up the richness of your life.

No matter how much sense this makes, we often find
ourselves trying to get back in control. Perhaps the hardest
thing for a person to do is to trust and let go. It never
happens without trusting in the one who walks towards
us over the waves. The power to let go is from God. It's
crucial to pray for it. And it helps quite a bit to look at the
lives of those who have learned how to let go. They can
teach us something. It even helps to look at ourselves, to
remember the times when we trusted enough to let go.
Were we better off in those times?

"You, Lord, give perfect peace to those who keep their
purpose firm and put their trust in you. Trust in the Lord
forever; he will always protect us" (Isaiah, 26:3-4). Can we
get hold of ourselves so that we might have the courage to
put our lives into the hands of God? Can we let go of the
fear that keeps us from trusting in God's guidance and
protection?

You know the difficulties I have in letting go and trusting
    in you, my God.
Help me to get hold of myself,
to let go of my fear of letting go.
I know that this is like asking for a miracle,
but I ask you confidently for this gift,
because how else can I live my life as you would have me
    live it?
And how can I love you if I'm afraid to put my life into
    your hands?

You know my weakness.
Fill me with your strength
that I might change the attitudes
that keep me from experiencing the joy of your presence.

Are there any fears or anxieties that you refuse to let go of? Try to become more aware of the damage these attitudes do to your life. The strength to let go does not come from you alone, but from God. Have you been hurt by trying to live by your own strength alone? Ask God for the faith to trust in his power so that you might put away your fears and live with greater freedom.

If we believe God is so good, why are we so afraid?

Luke presents the story of a rich man who wanted to follow Jesus. The man had lived a good life. He had obeyed all of the commandments, but still he asked Jesus if there were something more he could do. Jesus replied, "There is still one more thing you need to do. Sell all you have and give the money to the poor, and you will have riches in heaven; then come and follow me" (Luke 18:22).

The rich man went away sad. The price of following the invitation of Jesus seemed too high. What attitude might have motivated his refusal? At first glance, it might seem that possessiveness was the culprit. Perhaps the rich man felt that he was being asked to give up too much. Could there have been an even deeper cause, however, that prompted him to turn away from Jesus?

Suppose the rich man doubted that following Jesus could bring him greater happiness than his riches. The underlying attitude then would have been fear. A lack of trust in God would account for his refusal. Perhaps we can empathize with the rich man's plight. How would we feel about putting our lives totally at the disposal of God? In our finer moments, we might be prompted to say, "Do with me what you want, Lord." But then there is the afterthought. What if God really does with me what he wants to? What will he demand? Will I be worse off? What we really are afraid of is that somehow God will do us in. But if we really believe in God's love for us, how could we ever imagine that saying yes to God would bring us harm? Our deepest need for conversion may be the need to turn away from our fear. We need to believe that God's invitation to follow him brings joy and peace, that it brings gain and not loss.

The ending of this story about the rich man offers the possibility of hope in the midst of darkness and fear. After the rich man leaves, Jesus says, "It is much harder for a rich person to enter the Kingdom of God than for a camel to go through the eye of a needle" (Luke 18:25). That seems like a hopeless situation. But when the apostles ask if there is anyone then who can be saved, Jesus answers, "What is impossible for [humanity] is possible for God" (Luke 18:27).

We have to look at our fears and whatever other destructive attitudes we are most unwilling to give up. Perhaps we, too, walk away from Jesus saddened. What Jesus leaves us with, however, is a promise of hope. God can do within us what we cannot do by ourselves. God's power is within us because he loves us. In this divine power is our hope.

We may be fearful and flawed, but we have hope because we are loved. Because we believe we are loved, we learn to grow in our awareness of God despite our fears and flaws. As we are slowly healed, our consciousness grows into ever greater depths of love and trust. A change of awareness occurs within us. We become more alive.

This journey into trust has its difficult moments, and so we need to believe that the continuing change that can occur within ourselves is not our work alone. Many times we lose heart because we forget that. In many different ways, the Bible makes it clear that it is God who enables us to become what he has created us to be. Our growth is his work, and we bear no fruit without God's power within us, a power which always enables us to be more alive, more conscious, more awake.

The key to our growth is our willingness to leave some space for God to do his work within us. We are dependent upon God. Sometimes we forget this truth when we feel strong. We have to feel our own weakness to appreciate our need for God. Most of us can remember a difficult situation in life where we had to rely totally on God. Remembering those times of weakness when we are feeling strong reminds us of our need.

We must let God heal us from our fears. Rather than keep our distance from God because of fear, we need to take our fears to him. This is the first step. As God heals our fears, trust and generosity flow more easily into our relationship with God. God will be gentle with us, and his healing touch will make us free.

Fill me with confidence in you, my God,
so that I might trust the ways in which you lead me.
You are worthy of trust.
I know this intellectually,
but sometimes my emotions don't follow what my head
    knows to be true.
I don't know the reasons for this, my God,

but you know the split that is within me.

I seem to be attracted to you,

and at the same time, something within me pulls away.

It is your healing power that can finally change my faulty
    attitudes toward you.

Change me with your healing power,

and then my relationship with you will be filled with trust
    and joy.

❖ ❖ ❖ ❖ ❖

In what way are you like the rich man who refused to
trust himself to the path God pointed out for him? Identify
an area of your life which you seem most unwilling to
entrust to the providence of God. Does fear weaken your
ability to trust in God? Reflect on the words, "What is
impossible for [humanity] is possible for God" (Luke
18:27). Pray that this passage might be realized on a deeply
personal level in your life so that you might see your life's
possibilities in a new way.

If life's joys seem to elude us, maybe we need to change the way we look at life.

Now here's a hard one. Running a marathon might
seem easier than changing our own particular outlook on
life. We'd much prefer that other people would change
theirs. Of course, it would be great if we all changed
together. But the problem is that we have no control over
others. We do have some control over ourselves though,
and that's a good place to start. It is within ourselves that
we find the divine help to remove the obstacles than keep
us from becoming more deeply conscious.

Our attitudes have something to do with what we get
out of life because they determine the way we see our

possibilities. In the story of the presentation of Jesus in the temple (Luke 2:21-38), two people, Simeon and Anna recognize the uniqueness of Jesus as soon as they see him. The Bible tells us that these two people hungered to know God, and waited patiently until their expectation was fulfilled. Their attitude was one of searching and openness, and that is why it was possible for them to recognize Jesus. Had there been no openness, how could they have recognized him? And if there is no openness to recognizing the presence of God within ourselves and within the world around us, how can we become more conscious?

Removing the barriers to hope and openness makes it easier for us to realize what we would like to accomplish. Hope and openness enable us to see our possibilities. A friend of mine who ran a rehabilitation center told me the story of how he met his wife. He had put an ad in the local newspaper for a nurse, and when a young lady came in to apply for the job, my friend knew she was the one who was to be his wife. Instant recognition! They married, had a family, and are still happily living together. It was my friend's attitude of optimistic openness that enabled him to recognize the woman who was to be his wife. Without that openness, would he ever have recognized her? If he had been a pessimist, would he ever have asked her to marry him? The fear of a possible no might have paralyzed his vocal chords. Attitudes make all the difference. A prudent attitude of hope is part of the foundation for contentment in life. Without hope, there is no growth in our communion with God and with others.

Our experience of contentment and love also depends on our capacity to be comfortable with life's disappointments. If our attitude toward life is non-judgmental, in the sense that we avoid becoming bogged down by our likes and dislikes, then we become freer of feelings that disturb our peace.

A convalescent was praying in her home for sunshine. After three weeks of solid cloud cover and snow, she began to feel alternately depressed and angry. Finally, as the depression and anger deepened, she brought her feelings to God in prayer. "Why, God, why this unrelenting gloom and snow?" As she waited patiently, God answered her in the depths of her heart with the words, "'Tis so." Now those words might not seem to be very much of an answer. And yet, when the convalescing woman accepted the answer, her depression and anger gradually melted away. An attitude of true acceptance can liberate a person from many painful situations. When we stop fighting against life, against those things which can't be changed, contentment becomes more of a possibility. So does love. The changing of attitudes removes the barriers to fuller consciousness and opens up the possibility for new life. This all seems so reasonable. Why, then, do so many people seem to be stuck in non-accepting attitudes?

Well, for starters, it takes a deep sense of humility to change long established attitudes, to accept people and circumstances which go against our grain. Who can easily let go of the wish to have life run its course as he or she wants? Egos are at work here, and one of the most difficult things in the world to tame is the ego. When someone has succeeded in doing that, he or she has performed the equivalent of a miracle. The reward is a deeper sense of harmony and wholeness, a basic contentment in the midst of living with difficult situations that are beyond one's control.

The harmony and wholeness of our lives are God's gifts to us. Other people can encourage us to be whole. They can share valuable insights that are able to steer us toward wholeness. But the power to be selfless, the power to remove the attitudes that block our wholeness, this power comes from God. God, of course, wants to share this power with us, since his desire for us is that we should become fully awake. He has already put that power within us. We need simply to pray for the realization of what is always within.

"The Kingdom of God is within you" (Luke 17:21). In allowing God to remove the barriers to the kingdom within us, we become more fully alive.

I am stuck with attitudes that keep me from being more
   joyfully conscious, my God.
Help me to live my life with expectant hope,
and to avoid the depression and anger that sometimes
   arise when things don't go my way.
Free my mind so I might see the good things of life that I
   often overlook.
Open my eyes to the good so that I can see it before me.
Increase in me the gifts of insight and wholeness, my God.
You are the source of all these gifts,
and with them you enrich my life.

Is your life marked by hope? What attitude would you have to change in order to be more aware of the joys that life makes possible for you?

Life belongs to those who find the narrow gate.

Go in through the narrow gate, because the gate to hell is wide and the road that leads to it is easy, and there are many who travel it. But the gate to life is narrow and the way that leads to it is hard, and there are few people who find it (Matthew 7:13-14).

It seems that it is only with some difficulty that we remove the barriers that keep us from becoming more fully conscious. No wonder! Look at the price we have to pay. We can only find life when we stop spending so much energy on ourselves. Those who are willing to forget themselves are the ones who go through the narrow gate that leads to life. To accept without bitterness the suffering that is a part of life, to love those who seem unlovable, to serve others at some expense to ourselves—this is part of what it means to go through the narrow gate. In doing these things, we begin to resemble God, for we do what God does. God then recognizes us as people who are like him, as people who want to live as he lives, and do what he does. It is in God's recognition and acceptance of us that we find our security and our joy.

Going through the narrow gate means living a life of love that costs us something. The narrow gate offers discomfort to us because it squeezes our egos. For those with small egos, however, the narrow gate may not be that much of a problem. In the end, the journey through the narrow gate turns out to be the easier way. Love quickly becomes more fulfilling than selfishness.

There is a delightful series of books called *The Chronicles of Narnia*, written by C. S. Lewis. The stories deal with the struggle between good and evil as it unfolds in a distant land called Narnia. A lion named Aslan makes frequent appearances as the story develops. Aslan, an image of God, comes to explain why certain things happen the way they do, and to give his help to the people on Narnia when they need it. At the end of the *Chronicles*, the time comes for the world of Narnia to pass away. Before the end, its inhabitants must face Aslan one last time. They do so either with hatred or with love in their hearts. Those who face him with love find their way to his country through a narrow stable door. Those who hate or distrust him are left outside and disappear. Losing their chance for life, they are never heard from again.

Within ourselves there is a battle between selflessness and selfishness, between love and indifference, between consciousness and unconsciousness. We know the power of our own destructive attitudes along with their illusory attractiveness. They seem to offer us a sense of pleasure at times. Even revenge and hatred may offer us a fleeting, perverted sense of happiness. In the end, though, they do us in. Maybe this is what Jesus had in mind when he spoke of the wide gate that leads to that place where no one wants to go. But a person would not have to wait for hell to experience the pain of selfish living. The pain is quite real even in this life. It would seem, then, that only masochists would freely choose the wide gate, because it is a way of suffering. Our negative attitudes cause suffering, and eventually bring us to our own ruin.

We find life when we remove the obstacles to consciousness, when we put away all those attitudes and actions that keep us from being lovingly conscious of God and of our brothers and sisters. Whatever we do or think that keeps us from this kind of consciousness is really anti-life. And so we find that the wide gate and the narrow gate are antithetical. The wide gate is initially an easier way, but it leads to the suffering of being left only with oneself. The narrow gate is initially a harder way, but it leads to the joy of being one with God. The one who enters it finds what his or her life was always meant to be—a life of awareness that leads to unity with everything there is.

Grant me the courage, my God, to go through the
     narrow gate.
Help me develop a truly wide vision of human life,
so I can choose the narrow gate.

May I experience the joys of persevering in my passage
through the narrow gate in this life.
Help me to remember that the experience which begins in
this life will have its fruition in the next.
Help me to choose rightly in this life, my God.
You know, my God, how formidable are the obstacles
and how they play havoc with my attempts to make the
right choices.
I need a miracle to be free.
Will you consider me too rash if I count on you for one?

Examine yourself. Are there any parts of you so bloated
with egoism and selfishness that they can't get through the
narrow gate? Going through the narrow gate is initially a
painful experience, but can you see how it leads to a fuller,
more loving life? If you need a miracle to slim down the
ego, would you be willing to pray for one?

*Without an openness to miracles in our lives,
we lack the freedom to grow
in awareness of love.*

We read in the Bible that Jesus performed many
miracles and cures for those who had faith in his power.
The blind, the lame, the ill—all of these people suffered a
disability that they couldn't overcome through their own
power alone. They were powerless and had to rely on a
power that transcended their own. When they opened
themselves in faith to the healing power of God, they
experienced an influx of new life. This new life was a
foretaste of what they were to enjoy in the resurrected life.
It is the will of God that we should be healed from the

obstacles to a more conscious life, that we should be awake to love and aware of God's goodness in our lives. When we experience impediments to this awareness, there is always the possibility that a "miracle" can make us free. An openness to God's power and healing in our lives makes it possible for God to give us the healing that he wants us to enjoy. The following text beautifully expresses God's intention that we should be open to experience freedom from the impediments that keep us from being fully alive.

> Then Jesus . . . stood up to read the scriptures and was handed the book of the prophet Isaiah. He unrolled the scroll and found the place where it is written, "The Spirit of the Lord is upon me, because he has chosen me to bring good news to the poor. He has sent me to proclaim liberty to the captives and recovery of sight to the blind, set free the oppressed and announce that the time has come when the Lord will save his people."

> Jesus rolled up the scroll, gave it back to the attendant, and sat down. All the people in the synagogue had their eyes fixed on him, as he said to them, "This passage of scripture has come true today, as you heard it being read" (Luke 4:16-22).

Jesus' presence among his contemporaries was a healing presence that stretched their abilities to enjoy life and to live more fully. When Jesus calmed the storm that threatened the lives of the apostles (Mark 4:35-41) he demonstrated the power of God to bring order out of disharmony, to bring protection in the midst of chaos. In the raising of Lazarus (John 11:1-44) Jesus showed the power of God to bring life from what seemed dead. From death, God has the power to bring something vital and new. In the healing of the blind and deaf (Luke 7:21-22) Jesus showed God's power to restore human beings to a fuller mode of sensory consciousness, a symbol of the

deeper spiritual consciousness to which we are all called.
All of these miracles were given so that their recipients
could experience the goodness of God leading them to
deeper levels of conscious living. God freed them from the
obstacles that limited their lives.

What are we to say about the risen Jesus' presence
among us today? What expectation can we have that God's
power will touch our lives to free us from some of the
burdens that keep us from living more fully? The biblical
miracles tell us that God is a God who renews life, a God
who offers possibilities for awareness by healing us from
the impediments that shrink our lives. The healing will not
always be physical, of course. Many times the healing
consists in the strength to take life as it is, to live it lovingly
as we find it by accepting what cannot be changed. This
kind of acceptance is indeed a miracle for human nature,
and the benefits from this attitude toward life lead to fuller
life, the most powerful example being Jesus' acceptance of
his cross. From this acceptance, the human nature of Jesus
was raised by the Father to a resurrected life. God brings
about new life from death, hope from hopelessness, meaning from chaos. We may expect to experience some aspects
of this transformation even in this life.

The gospel points out the relationship between faith
and healing. With the attitude of faith, we can be open to
the surprises that touch our lives when we least expect
them. We should always be prepared for them, for the
curing touch of God comes more easily to those who wait
hopefully with open hands. These healing surprises are a
hint, a kind of foretaste of the wholeness and integration
we will all experience when we pass from this life into the
dimension of the resurrected life.

We experience these healing surprises through intuitions that come to us, intuitions that give us new ways of
looking at life that make us more joyful and free. These

healing intuitions are gifts of the Spirit. The healing may come as a release from fear, sadness, pessimism, in short, from a whole host of negative attitudes that restrict our joyful awareness of life. New possibilities open up to us, possibilities which previously seemed hidden. The God who brings life from death, order from chaos, is the God who brings wholeness in this life to those who earnestly desire and seek it. When we are touched by the God who wills our wholeness, we come to understand another dimension of what it means to call God our Savior.

It is the Holy Spirit within us who teaches us which miracles we need to pray for. In the quietness of our minds, God breathes into us the inspiration to pray for the healing that he wills us to receive. In this way, we cooperate with God's healing power. We cannot do this, however, without a quiet, faithful listening, an openness to the Spirit of God who finds his own way of communicating himself to us. With faith, patience, and prayer, we find our own way to discover how God does communicate with us. The discovery can happen at any time and in any place if we are prepared by cultivating a quiet mind which is open to God's healing touch. The Spirit comes and goes as it wills. We need to be ready and waiting.

I long for your healing touch in my life, my God,
but you know better than I how much I need it.
And you know the particular kind of healing I need.
The healing miracles in the gospel are signs of your love,
and I hope for these signs in my own life.
You see how I am chained by the negative emotions that
    grip me like so many addictions.
In your loving kindness, set me free

so that I might enjoy the fullness of life that you wish me
   to have.
I also make this prayer for all of my brothers and sisters,
   my God.
My wholeness will not be complete unless they are made
   whole too.
Through your healing touch, give us a foretaste of the
   resurrected life to which you call us.
Through your healing touch, let us experience even now
   something of that life.
Thank you, my God, for your love which sets us free.

What is the miracle in your life that you most need to
pray for? What could you do to add to the possibility of
its realization?

Alive Throughout the Ages to Come

"What happens to us when we die?" the people asked. "Is it really true that we are reborn into a new life?"

"Of course it's true," the teacher replied. "Could you ever imagine a caring God who would give you life and love, and then take it all away?"

> Jesus said, "I am the resurrection and the life. Whoever believes in me will live, even though he dies; and whoever lives and believes in me will never die. Do you believe this?"
>
> —John 11:25-26

*The journey of consciousness begins in this life,
but its fulfillment is only experienced in the
new life of the resurrection.*

Christians believe that they are saved through the death and resurrection of Jesus Christ. Part of God's gift of salvation is freedom from the constraints of space and time, which is what the resurrection implies. We discover God in the present moment, but because the present moment is situated in space and time, it limits our discovery. Our seeing in space and time is necessarily veiled and incomplete. Clarity comes only when we pass from this life to the next. This is the life to which Jesus ultimately calls us, his own resurrected life.

> "There are many rooms in my Father's house, and I am going to prepare a place for you. I would not tell you this if it were not so. And after I go and prepare a place for you, I will come back and take you to myself, so that you will be where I am" (John 14:2-3).

The promise of resurrection, the fullness of life that never ends, is the magnificent promise that Jesus makes to all of us. The promise is magnificent because it is God's pledge that we will enjoy a lasting, fully conscious union with him and with his entire creation. This union will be the ultimate experience that constitutes our complete fulfillment. It is the experience for which we were made, from the very first moment that God caused us to be. The completion of consciousness will be given to us through our resurrection into eternal life, when we will join all of those who have been liberated from the present constraints of space and time through the power of Jesus Christ.

We tend to look at the resurrected life as a great mystery, and of course it is. The life to come transcends our imagination. But does that mean that we can't surmise anything about the resurrected life? And if we can, what is it that we can surmise? Are there some experiences in our present life that give a hint about what the resurrected life might be? These aren't useless questions, because when we look at them, we discover the fuller meaning of our present life. The discovery we make is this: the seeds of the resurrected life are already to be found in the present moment, because we already have some ability to be lovingly conscious of reality. When we are born into the resurrected life, those seeds grow into complete fruition.

We long for this fullness of life even now, although the longing sometimes shows itself in distorted ways. Is there anyone who does not yearn for a deeper sense of meaning and fulfillment than he or she already has? It is this longing that will finally be satisfied as we pass through this life into the resurrected one. The hope for what is to come should be a source of joy for us even now, for even now this life can teach us something, although in a very incomplete and shadowy way, about the joys of the resurrected life to come.

My God, I thank you for the fullness of what I am,
and for the fullness of what you have called me to be.
May I live each moment as consciously as I can,
and come to understand that each moment points to
    something beyond itself.
You are present in every aspect of my life,
revealing yourself to me,
drawing me on to the marvelous completeness of the
    resurrection.

It is there that you promise to satisfy all of the longings for
    fullness of life
that are so much a part of my being.

Do you look at God's promise of resurrected life with a
sense of fear or disinterest, or do you look at it with a sense
of joy? How would an increased hope for the resurrected
life add a new dimension of joy to your present life?

*All of us are born twice: once from the wombs
of our mothers into this world, and then from
the womb of this world into the resurrected life.*

Birth from the wombs of our mothers into this world,
birth from the womb of this world into resurrected life—
each of these births results in a transformed life. The
fetus lives quite differently after his birth into this world
than he did during life in the womb of his mother. The
resurrected person lives quite differently after her birth
into eternity than she did during her life in the womb of
this world. The resurrected person and the fetus are both
born into new life. When the fetus leaves the womb, we
call it birth. When someone leaves the womb of this
world, we call it death. Why is that? Why can't we simply say that people who die haven't really died, but that
they have been transformed, born into eternal life? Such
people are quite fully alive. They have merely died to the
constraints of space and time, to the incomplete way in
which they experienced life on earth. But after their birth
into eternity, they become more fully alive because of the
new way in which they live. Couldn't one say something
similar about the fetus? The fetus dies to the constraints
of the womb, to the life experienced within the mothers.

But once born into the world, the child is more fully alive in a new way of living.

A wonderful continuity exists between all stages of life—life in the womb, life in the world, and life in eternity. One stage evolves into the other. Such is the magnificent plan of God. The resurrected life is the fruit of the life that begins in the womb. Just as it would make no sense for the fetus not to be born into the world, so it would make no sense for people in this world not to be born into eternity.

When you observe a fetus closely, you know that it is ultimately designed for an environment other than the womb. Its physical make-up tells you that. You see the arms, the legs, the eyes, the mouth—physical equipment that says that the fetus isn't made for an extended stay in the womb, but that it is destined for a life to be lived elsewhere. Without birth into the world as a goal, the physical characteristics of the fetus would make no sense.

And what about us who are living in the womb of this world? If we take a close look at ourselves, what can we intuit regarding our ultimate destiny? The swift aging of our bodies tells us that our hold on earthly life is short. Through aging as well as through the many accidents which occur in life, our bodies speak to us of impermanence, and yet, something within the human spirit longs for permanence. While these longings of themselves are not proofs of our eternal destiny, they do tell us that we are not really at home in this world.

Our longings suggest to us that our destiny lies elsewhere. Many cultures celebrate this intuition in the way they conduct their burial ceremonies. They prepare themselves physically and spiritually for the journey beyond time. The idea of eternity is a part of humankind's sense of reality. Many people sense the truth of this in their lives and celebrate it in their religions. And for those of us who believe in the revelation of God, we know that our ultimate destiny transcends space and time, and that it is bound up with the God in whose life we share.

I know that my life in this world will eventually come to
     an end, my God,
and that it is only a part of the evolution of my entire life.
May I not be afraid of death—the passage to fuller life.
When it comes, may I welcome it with joy,
for it will lead me to the fullness of life,
the marvelous gift you have offered me
from the moment I was born.

How do you experience the impermanence of your life? What longings for permanence and transcendence do you experience? Do you ever feel a sense of awe about this life, and yet realize that your deepest longings can only be realized in the life to come?

*For those who know how to look, the reality of
the resurrected life can be known,
in shadow form, even in this life.*

While the resurrected life must always remain a mystery to us, we are capable of intuiting something about it through images in nature and through our own life experience. Perhaps the most powerful image of transformation in nature is the butterfly. A butterfly, of course, is simply a transformed caterpillar. But for those who believe in the resurrected life, it is an image that can speak powerfully of what happens to them through death and resurrection.

Caterpillars appear to have a fairly pleasant life. Their major challenge is to remain undetectable to their predators, and from the proliferation of transformed caterpillars, it seems that many of them do. The caterpillar feasts on an almost inexhaustible salad bar available right under its feet. There's plenty to eat, and plenty of time simply to bask in the sunshine, an experience that we ourselves probably long for at times. The caterpillar never gets very far or sees very much, but nature generally takes good care of it. To a caterpillar who escapes the beak of the bird or the sting of the wasp, life may not seem bad at all.

One day, however, the caterpillar begins to spin a series of threads around itself. When it finishes the spinning, it is enclosed in a cocoon, a structure that almost seems to resemble a miniature tomb. Initially, as it experiences the darkness, the former caterpillar might ask itself, is this all there is? After a pleasant life of eating and basking in the sunshine, is this all that remains—nothingness and darkness? But slowly a change begins to take place, and one day the tomb-like cocoon opens to reveal a creature that has been totally transformed, something that has been made quite beautiful.

If this newly transformed butterfly could think as humans do, it might say something like this: "I look so different. Everything around me looks so different. I can see plants and flowers that I never saw before. This is tremendous! And what are these two shiny membranes attached to my body? They're beautiful. Look at those colors. But what are these things for?"

The butterfly moves its two shiny wings and immediately it soars into the air. Where the caterpillar noticed only the surfaces of leaves, the butterfly sees the entire garden. Where the caterpillar chewed on plants, the butterfly unfolds its proboscis and feasts on nectar. Its way of being is completely transformed. And yet if you forget about the wings and look closely at the butterfly's body, you can see a faint vestige of the caterpillar.

Perhaps we should see this whole evolution from caterpillar to butterfly as an image of our own transformation. In our earthly existence, we are somewhat like the caterpillar. In our resurrected state, we are more like the butterfly. The image speaks powerfully, but is there something more that can be surmised about our resurrected state?

In the course of our daily lives, we experience various states of conscious awareness. Usually, we experience ourselves as separate from others and from the world in which we live. We see ourselves as different from one another, and that, in part, defines for us who we are. But it is also the kind of consciousness which allows us to manipulate one another, and to ignore those with whom we feel no bond. It is the kind of consciousness that breeds loneliness. Family ties and bonds with those who share common experiences help to alleviate our loneliness, although we rarely experience a sense of complete unity with those we love. But if we've ever had an experience of total unity with someone, then we've already known in a veiled way something of what we shall enjoy forever in the resurrected state with everyone.

An example of total unity comes from a story shared by one of my former students. After I finished a lecture on the meaning of silence in Buddhism, the student came up to my desk and said, "Father, I had the best time with my girl last night." I wasn't sure what this had to do with the context of the lecture, but the young man quickly cleared up the mystery. He and his girl friend sat in a car in a park, and for half an hour, neither of them said a word. They just sat quietly in one another's presence. The young man had lost all sense of awareness of himself. He was fully present to the person he loved, and in the experience he became one with her. At that moment, he wasn't thinking about his relationship with her, nor was he evaluating his experience. He was simply present to her as she was.

Perhaps some of us have had a similar experience sometime in our lives. It might have been with another person. It might have been with something in nature. It might have been with God. What characterizes such an experience is the sense of immediacy. There is no barrier of thought standing between you and the experience. You don't think about the person in an analytical way, but you directly experience the presence of the person in an intuitive way. It is an experience of transcendence. And the whole experience fills you with a great peace and joy.

Much of our usual state of consciousness in this life is characterized by desire for what we want, and by fear of what we want to avoid. In other words, our state of consciousness revolves around ourselves. To the extent that it does, we find it difficult to experience deeply what is not ourselves. And much of our consciousness revolves around thinking about things, rather than experiencing them directly in themselves. Our thoughts and concepts can become barriers to experiencing our lives. We think about life, but frequently don't live it. We are often like the traveler who stands in front of a beautiful cathedral while his mind is on his business back home. If we live life like that, we separate ourselves from life's joys.

In the resurrected life, our experiences will not revolve around ourselves, nor will we have concepts about God. We will know directly, perhaps somewhat like the young man who experienced the presence of his girl friend

without words and without concepts. Just the direct experiencing!

> What we see now is like a dim image in a mirror; then
> we shall see face-to-face. What I know now is only
> partial; then it will be complete—as complete as God's
> knowledge of me. Meanwhile these three remain:
> faith, hope, and love; and the greatest of these is love
> (1 Corinthians 13:12-13).

Because of my blindness, Lord,
I often fail to grasp that the resurrected life is already
    present in a veiled way,
right in the midst of my earthly life.
While paying full attention to this life,
I want to discover in it the traces of the life to come.
How can I find my full meaning
if I fail to make this discovery?
May I come to experience,
as well as I can in this present life,
something of the fullness which is yet to come.

Think about the image of the caterpillar and the butterfly. How does this image relate to your hope in the
resurrected life?

Transcendent experiences are those that take us out of
our ordinary state of consciousness and open us to deeper
levels of awareness that go beyond our usual way of
understanding. Feelings of oneness with those we love or
with nature are examples of this kind of awareness. How
have you experienced examples of this in your life?

In the resurrected life, we shall be completely free from the restrictions of space and time.

Our ultimate salvation is to be free from the barriers that keep us from loving and experiencing union with God and with our brothers and sisters. But salvation also includes freedom from the restrictions of space and time. Don't we all long for this? In the resurrected life, how will we experience this kind of freedom?

> Then I saw a new heaven and a new earth. The first heaven and the first earth disappeared, and the sea vanished. And I saw the Holy City, the new Jerusalem, coming down out of heaven from God, prepared and ready, like a bride dressed to meet her husband. I heard a loud voice speaking from the throne: "Now God's home is with [humankind]! He will live with them, and they shall be his people. God himself will be with them, and he will be their God. He will wipe away all tears from their eyes. There will be no more death, no more grief or crying or pain. The old things have disappeared." Then the one who sits on the throne said, "And now I make all things new!" He also said to me, "Write this, because these words are true and can be trusted" (Revelation 21:1-5).

To be free from the restrictions of space and time means, in part, to be free from pain and death. If we were not freed from these, then the resurrected life would perhaps be little different from our present life. But God promises to make all things new. Buried with Christ in baptism, we receive the power to be born into a totally new kind of life where there is no room for death. No more separation from those we love! No longer that temporal veil that keeps us from the clear vision of God, from the experience of blissful oneness with God and with those we love. The union will be complete and unbreakable. There will be no possibility of loss. And that will be our joy.

We will be free from the heaviness that limits us to confined areas of space. Being free from the heaviness of matter, we will be wherever our thoughts take us. The entire universe will be our home, and all of its parts will be open to us. Though the caterpillar crawled, the butterfly will soar. Our freedom will be marvelously complete. The possibilities of such a life defy the imagination, but these possibilities all flow from the nature of the resurrected life, a spiritual life that is free from the restrictions of space and time.

This freedom does not exclude some kind of connection with the material universe. Knowing it, loving it, and being in it will constitute a part of our complete happiness. It will be a part of our lives. Our experience of total joy will include the awareness and love of the material universe, but in a way that leaves us free from being affected by its change and impermanence. In the Christian understanding of resurrection, there will always be some kind of connection between the transformed person and the experience of bodiliness, between spirit and body. What kind of body this is must remain a mystery, but St. Paul was not afraid to say something about this, even in the face of the mystery.

> Someone will ask, "How can the dead be raised to life? What kind of body will they have?" You fool! When you plant a seed in the ground, it does not sprout to life unless it dies. And what you plant is a bare seed, perhaps a grain of wheat or some other grain, not the full-bodied plant that will later grow up. God provides that seed with the body he wishes; he gives each seed its own proper body.... This is how it will be when the dead are raised to life. When the body is buried, it is mortal; when raised, it will be immortal. When buried, it is ugly and weak; when raised, it will be beautiful and strong. When buried, it is a physical body; when raised, it will be a spiritual body (1 Corinthians 15:35-38, 42-44).

We are left with a magnificent hope, with the promise of our ultimate maturity and fulfillment. We are destined to be transformed. The caterpillar will be changed into the butterfly, becoming what it was always meant to be from the first moment of its life.

Your generosity, my God, is more than I can comprehend.
You fulfill all of my deepest desires for life and union.
You make my being whole,
and I discover that you and I are entwined in an eternal
     embrace.
You show me the universe, the work of your hands,
and I will always be a part of it.
Yet, through the gift of resurrection, I shall be freed
from the restrictions of space and time that characterize
     my life in the universe as it presently is.
Resurrected life!
That is your gift to me, my God,
and your gift to all my brothers and sisters.
Through this gift, may we all experience eternal union
     with each other
and thank you for the shared gift of your life.

Some connection with the matter of the universe will be a part of our resurrected experience. What does this say to you about the value of your body, and about the necessity of treating our planet with respect? Do you see your body along with the matter of this world as holy and precious in God's sight?

*In the resurrected life, we will not be strangers
to one another. We will recognize one another,
and the friendships that began in this life
will continue into the next.*

If the resurrected life is a life of love, that love would
have to include our relationships with one another. Would
our experience of resurrected life be complete for us
without this? If there is to be a continuation of relationships with those we love, there must be a way for us to
recognize one another. We would be unable to love what
we could not recognize. How this recognition can take
place must, of course, remain a mystery. But in some way,
the memories and experiences of each one of us will have
to be transparent to all of those who care to notice. Our
memories and experiences help define who we are and
will enable others to recognize us. It is the uniqueness of
our own experiences, past and present, that characterize
our identity and reveal to others who we are.

Imagine looking at a film. What we see impressed on
the film actually took place some time in the past, even
though everything seems to be taking place in the present
as we watch. Films differ from one another according to
what has been recorded on them. In a similar way, our
personalities are formed according to what has been
recorded on them. No two recordings are the same. That
is what makes us different and recognizable.

In the resurrected life, people will recognize one
another's personalities intuitively, without the aid of
physical signs. Even in this life, some people have intuitions about others that do not always seem to be based
primarily on physical signs. In the resurrected life, intuitive recognition of one another would be the foundation
on which love and friendship would continue to grow.

There will be nothing static in our experience of resurrected life. Our experience of God and of the entire created
universe will continue to grow. We will never fully comprehend God nor the entirety of creation which continuously flows from God's hands. The longer we gaze,
the more our understanding and joy will increase. Since
the possibilities of growth are unlimited, the resurrected
life will never seem boring to us. There will never be an
end to what we can experience.

Based on differences in our personalities, all of us will
probably understand God and his creation in different
ways, just as people see and appreciate this life in a
variety of ways. And so we will be able to learn from
others. We will be able to intuit their experiences, sharing
what we learn with one another. The fruits of this kind
of sharing are endless. In the resurrected life, this sharing
will be effortless. It will be the direct result of the
friendship that we will share with one another. Everything that we know, everything that we are will be completely transparent. We will simply look at one another
and see who each one is, and know what each one
knows. Everything we are will be shared with complete
openness and love.

This idea raises an interesting question. If our personalities are formed by our past experiences, and if the
traces of the past are open for others to see, will our past
sinfulness be known? From an egoistic point of view, just
the mere thought of that might be discomforting. It might
seem better that past sinfulness should be hidden. Better
to keep the skeletons in the closet. Wouldn't we blush a
little if our full past were known?

Suppose, though, that our past ignorance and sinfulness revealed to others how God's love overcame all of our
negativities and saved us. Suppose our past sinfulness
revealed how the healing touch of God had transformed

our lives. It would be clear then how the power of God healed each one of us and made us whole. Our past sinfulness would not be seen as shameful, but as a state of suffering that was healed by the creative mercy of God. If we looked at our past sinfulness in this way, we might want it to be known to others. For those past sins would reveal the power of a healing, loving God. We would want others to know what God had done for us.

Such an attitude, of course, would not be possible if we were controlled by our egos. An ego state of consciousness always asks what is best for itself. It sees itself as separate from God and others, and it looks first of all to its own good. But in the resurrected life, we will see ourselves as one with God and with others. If that is the case, there will be no room for preoccupation with ourselves. There will be only an outpouring of who we are, a giving of ourselves to others as we are. And we will be delighted that others can see in us how God's mercy and love made us whole, bringing health where before there had been sickness. Such an attitude might be somewhat incomprehensible to us now, but then we're talking about an "ego-less" state, the way we will be in the life to come.

My God, you know how important my friends are to me, and how painful it would be for me to be parted from them.

But in your love, you give us to each other eternally.

In our unconditional love for one another, we mirror your love for us.

In our intuitive knowledge of one another, we know after the manner of your knowing.

In learning from one another's experiences of you, we grow in our knowledge of who you are.

Thank you, God, for my friends.
Thank you for friendship that lasts beyond space and time.
Thank you for the full promise of the resurrected life,
which you give to all those who wish to receive it.
Help me to believe in the resurrected life,
and never to fear the gaze
of your penetrating and all-accepting love.

If you believe that your friendships are eternal, how does this belief affect the way you regard your friendships in the present moment?

Friendship in the resurrected life can be shared fully only by those who can accept unconditional love.

In this life, belief in the unconditional love of others enables us to show others who we really are without fear of rejection. What about those who are afraid to reveal themselves? They exclude themselves from the full sharing of friendship. In their fear of being known, they choose isolation. Perhaps something similar happens in the resurrected life. Those who don't want their past to be known will experience isolation, until they grow out of their fear and are able to trust. Would their isolation be their purgatory?

Perhaps part of the meaning of purgatory is the refusal to be known. There may be some who would not want to be totally transparent to others. Because of their past sinfulness, they might have difficulty in trusting that they are loveable. Liberation from purgatory comes with the ability to trust. People will be free when they trust in God's unconditional love. They will be free when they trust in the unconditional love of all those who are resurrected. Finally, when they learn to trust, they will feel free to join the celestial party, to become one in love and friendship.

We experience something of this dynamic even in our earthly life. Haven't we all had the experience of going to a party where most of the people were strangers? We probably felt uncomfortable until we got to know them. The whole process took some trust. Our trust eventually allows us to go out to others, and perhaps then we begin to find that the party is at least an endurable experience. As the party continues, maybe we even grow to enjoy it and to make new friends who later enrich our lives. But had we chosen to remain on the sidelines, the party might have been a disturbing experience. Perhaps it will be similar at the party of the resurrected in eternity. Purgatory will be our choice not to trust and love, not to open ourselves to the loving, accepting gaze of others. What will finally save us is our trust in unconditional love, a trust made possible through the grace of God. As we might already know, that is no easy task. But it is a task which God, through the power of his presence, makes possible for us.

Since this process of growing toward unconditional love takes place beyond time, it probably makes no sense to ask how long it takes. What is important is that we become purified, completely free to give and receive unconditional love. Thus we finally reach the wholeness which God means for us to have.

My God, there is so much of me that I am reluctant to
    reveal.
And yet, all things are open to you,
so you already know who I am.

You tell me that I am loveable as I am.

Help me to believe this.

Help me to trust prudently in those who love me,

so that I can be open with them and believe in their
acceptance of me.

May my growth in trust begin now,

and may it come to completion in eternity.

Your promise of resurrected life is magnificent, my God.

Your unconditional love lasts forever

and reveals itself in ever more wonderful ways in the
resurrected life.

Why then am I so afraid when I realize that I will have to
leave this life?

Do you experience a sense of isolation in your life
because of a refusal to accept unconditional love? Even
though you may have been hurt in the past, can you
deepen your trust in the unconditional love of those who
genuinely love you now? Can you see how this trust leads
to a foretaste of the resurrected life? How many of your
fears would disappear if you were able to trust fully in the
reality of unconditional love?

If the resurrected life is such a magnificent gift, why are we so reluctant to let go of this life?

Perhaps our attitudes about eternal life are well
summed up by the following story. An angel appears to a
ball player and says, "I have good news and bad news. The
good news is that you've been picked for the all-star team
in heaven."

"Why that's great news," the player replies. "But what's the bad news?"

"The bad news," says the angel gravely, "is that the game starts in ten minutes."

We laugh at the story, and perhaps we do so with the knowledge that the story reflects something of our own attitudes about life. The promise of the resurrected life sounds fine in theory, but we are not overly eager for its fulfillment. In fact, we might actually fear its realization.

Just imagine for a moment that the fetus had a will of its own and could decide to remain in the womb. Perhaps the fetus, not having had any experience of life in the world, might prefer to stay with what it knows. The environment in the womb certainly has its pluses. Everything is provided—automatically controlled temperature, a continually open snack bar—in short, a cushioned existence. Being born has its uncomfortable moments. There's the slap on the backside to aid in the process of getting the first breath into the lungs. And perhaps the first breath of air carries with it its own discomfort.

Fortunately, the fetus does not have to make a choice. Nature makes it for her. And what nature does is wise, for birth is the passage to a whole array of joys that could never be found in the womb. A choice against birth would be a choice against sunsets, flowers, Beethoven, human friendships, and the knowledge of God's love. To experience the beginning of life's deeper joys, we have to be born.

We are in an intermittent stage between fetal existence and the resurrected life. This intermittent stage is not a bad life. In fact, there is much beauty in it. But we are caterpillars waiting to become butterflies. To want to settle down in this intermittent stage of life is to deny that the resurrected life is truly a magnificent promise. Of course, accepting this statement demands faith, hope, and love. But if these are difficult for us, we have a God who is willing to help us whenever we open our hearts to receive what he wants to give.

Accepting the promise of resurrected life with joy presupposes an ability to travel lightly in this life. If we are too attached to the present moment, we'll experience some discomfort in giving it up. But everything about this present moment is impermanent. Is there anything that isn't? The material things that we find so important either become useless or else we tire of them. Our youth and health are always impermanent realities. Our happiness comes and goes. Most of the things we treasure are subject to change.

Perhaps it is this aspect of our lives that we find the most disconcerting. We want to hang on to what we think is important. Wise people discover that there is nothing to hang on to. Life and love are gifts from God that we always possess, now and throughout eternity. They will always be there, so there is no need to hang on to them. All other things are impermanent, so it makes no sense to hang on to them either. In complete freedom from fear, we can let our lives evolve until they blossom into the resurrected life. Whatever our thoughts about this might be, this evolution is going to happen to us. Instead of fearing the process, we might as well learn to be comfortable with it and to see it for the gift of love which it is. With faith in God's promises, we can say to ourselves that the best is yet to come.

My God, your promise to us of continuous life is one that you must have made with joy.
Forgive us for the times when we have not received it
   with joy.

When those we love die,

we mourn for them just as you did for Lazarus.

Of course, you expect us to mourn,

but help us to see that the mourning we do is for ourselves,

and not for those who have been reborn into new life.

May we not fear the promises you make to us and to those
  we love.

Instead, may we live each moment in this life with trust.

May we be willing to let each moment go,

knowing that all of our earthly moments are leading us to
  the fullness of the resurrected life,

where everything within us will be brought to completion.

If the angel who appeared to the ball player were to
come to you with a similar message, how would you feel?
Can you think of any material possession or personal
relationship in your life that is not destined either to pass
away or to be transformed?

Dying is nothing new. We do it all the time.

What is life but a series of deaths, letting go that we
might be born into something new? The fetus dies to the
life in the womb, that it might be born into this world. And
once in this world, the child dies to being a child, that he
might be born into adolescence. The adolescent dies to
being an adolescent in order to be born into adulthood.
And then the adult dies to various stages of adulthood in
order to be born into old age. One who accepts this inevitable process becomes wise, because there is no birth
and growth without death. Life leads to death; death leads

to life. When we become conscious of this process, we understand the meaning of Jesus' words:

> "I am telling you the truth: a grain of wheat remains no more than a single grain unless it is dropped into the ground and dies. If it does die, then it produces many grains. Whoever loves his own life will lose it; whoever hates his own life in this world will keep it for life eternal" (John 12:24-25).

Throughout the journey of life, we die to incomplete ways of looking at life and we are born to an ever growing sense of wisdom. At least that is the ideal. For those who grow old optimally that is what actually happens. Perhaps we have experienced this growing sense of wisdom in our own lives. Can't we say that our outlook on life is more mature and satisfying now than when we were younger? Through a process of dying and rising, we have grown into a more complete way of loving and being.

Dying and rising have many facets. All through life, we are called to die to selfishness that we might rise to a life of greater love. It is a daily process. If we are open to the realities of growth and wholeness, we are no strangers to the dying that we call letting go. Without that kind of dying, we never grow up. But our final experience of growing up does not take place in this life. That happens to us through a process of dying and rising which brings us into resurrected life—our destiny from the moment we are born. All the daily dying and rising that we do in this life leads to that wonderful destiny. In the resurrected life, our consciousness is brought to fullness. The resurrected life is where we were always meant to be, and every moment of our lives is meant to lead us to it. Those who believe this have the courage to let go of this life that they might be reborn into the fullness of what they are called to be.

Keep me, my God, from hanging on when I should be
  letting go.
Teach me to avoid grasping on to my life.
Give me the faith to let go
so that I might grow into something new.
In letting go, I will possess the fullness of the life you
  created me to have.
Every experience of dying is a participation in your cross,
but if I have the courage to embrace your cross and make
  it mine,
you promise a new rising.
May I not hold back.
May I trust in your love
that reveals its depth by always calling me to deeper life.

Reflect on the many experiences of dying and rising that
have already occurred in your life. Did the end results of
these experiences bring you a deeper sense of wholeness
and joy? Can you see the daily process of dying and rising
as a journey leading to an ever fuller life and to a deeper
realization of God's love?

God's promise of resurrection is the ultimate revelation of his complete love for us.

Through the promise of the resurrection, it is as if God
were saying to us, "I love you so much that I want you
with me always. There never will be a time when I will
stop wishing you to exist. And so, I give you the power to

live eternally, and to soar with me as a butterfly soars in the wind."

When we marry, or when we make a solemn vow, the intention is to be faithful for life. Love enables us to have such intentions. For one who loves, anything less would be inconceivable. If our love can be this way, it should be easy for us to accept that God's love could be no less faithful and complete. His utter faithfulness is what comes across to us in his promise of eternal life.

This faithfulness is a promise to preserve us in all of our uniqueness. God's love respects the personality of each one whom he has created. The resurrected life will not do away with our individuality. If it did, what was resurrected would not really be us. The consequences of this are important. What is best in us, what is most authentically ourselves, all of this is preserved and raised up into everlasting life. Nothing important about us will be lost because God loves the totality of who we are.

Because we are all destined for unending life, we all have tremendous value in the sight of God. It is a further reason why we should treasure our relationships with one another. If, as we have seen earlier, human relationships last beyond the barriers of space and time, their value is inestimable. Human life itself is inestimable. God's promise of resurrected life guarantees the fullness of our worth and the eternal continuation of the human community. Understanding that our lives and relationships are eternal, we value each other all the more. As God pledges himself to us with an eternal embrace, so we pledge ourselves to the entire human family, with whom we shall all be as one.

I thank you, my God,
that your fidelity toward me is without limit.

Not only have you come into my life,
but you have invited me into yours.
And your invitation is not just for a time, but for eternity.
Our present life grows into the resurrected life.
It is in your gift of endless life
that I most clearly see your unlimited love.
May I learn to treasure more deeply what you promise,
and to treasure the entire human family
with a love that transcends the limits of space and time.

God's solemn promise is that you will be loved eternally. Does a reflection on this promise deepen your understanding of the immensity of God's love for you? Does this promise deepen your appreciation of all peoples with their diversities of races, cultures, and creeds? How might this promise increase your desire to build stronger communities of love right where you are in this present moment?

> *The resurrected life is not a radical break
> from this life. There is an
> intimate connection between the two.*

There is a charming story that makes this point by supposing a vague similarity between heaven and hell. According to the story, people in heaven and hell each sit at tables loaded with delicious food. Everything imaginable that is good to eat can be found there. The only difference is that the people in heaven are eating and having a good time, while the people in hell remain hungry as they sit frustrated in silence. The reason? Well, there is a rule that the people both in heaven and hell must observe. Eating must be done with five foot forks, and the forks must be held by the ends of their handles. Now the people in heaven figured out how to get around this obstacle. They knew instinctively that if they reached across the table and fed their neighbors, then everyone would be able to enjoy the feast. Such a solution would never occur to the people in hell, of course. They were too much focused on themselves. As a result, they all remained hungry.

The point? As we are in this life, so shall we be as we enter into the next. How could it be otherwise? This gives a whole new meaning to our present moment. The present moment has value in itself, but it also has value in relation to what it will become. We are the sum total of thousands and thousands of moments. This present moment is the result of all the choices of the past. The strength or weakness of our love in the present moment is determined by those choices. And the result of those choices is what we take with us into eternal life.

Perhaps we tend to think of our choices simply as they effect our temporal life. But that is only part of the picture. A global view of our lives reveals something else. Every act in the present prepares for the future. That is what makes the present so important.

You give me the gift of choice, my God,
and through my choices, you allow me to form my life.
You allow me to shape my future.
Each moment you give to me is beautiful in itself,
but each moment points to something beyond itself.
Help me to live well in the present moment,
so that my resurrected life might be lived in your presence.

If everything you do has its ramifications for your resurrected life, how does that deepen your appreciation for everything you do in the present moment? Whatever you do influences the formation of your personality and determines the quality of your future. In light of that, is there some particular direction in your life that you would like to change?

Live in the present; hope in the future.

Only by joining hope in the future with the immediacy of the present can we live full lives, open to the totality of what we are meant to be. Psychologists challenge us to live fully in the present moment. That challenge has been a core idea of this book. But can one live fully in the present moment and, at the same time, be dynamically awake to the promise of the future?

Many years ago several students and I drove nonstop from the University of Notre Dame to California. As we drove through the mountains of Utah, I was struck by their stark beauty. I thoroughly enjoyed that experience, and the memory is still with me. But while traveling through the mountains and savoring their beauty, I was aware that on the next day, I would again see my friends in California. In fact, that was the main reason for the trip. Awareness of the present and awareness of the future—both were integral parts of this journey to the west.

If we are people of hope, we live with joyful expectation for the promise of the resurrected life, even as we live dynamically in the midst of this life. Each moment of our present life slowly evolves toward death, which is our passage into the resurrected life. Although each moment of this life has its own value if we live it well, yet each moment is impermanent. We should be conscious of each moment, but always be willing to let it go and be open to where it leads us. The present moment is always changing into something else. It flows like a river whose waters we can never grasp in our hands. If we believe that our lives flow toward something ultimately fulfilling, then we are people of hope. We believe that each moment leads toward God's promise of resurrected life. And so we live fully in the present moment, with our hearts set on the promise of what is yet to come.

People who have this kind of faith will enjoy life in a much fuller way than those who don't. There is another dimension to their consciousness. They live not only in the present, but their awareness also includes the future with all of its rich possibilities of fulfillment. And if the present moment is a painful one, hope tells them that their future will be quite different. Even the fact of death can be faced with a lessening of fear. The promise of the resurrected life enables them to die with a hope for the future where impermanence is changed into fulfillment and where brokenness is transformed into wholeness. The stronger one's faith in the resurrected life, the less is one's fear of death. And for those who believe in the resurrected life, even their mourning for their loved ones is tinged with hope. For they know that their loved ones are made whole and joyful in the eternal embrace of God.

I thank you, my God, for this present moment
and for the promise to which it leads.
I thank you for the fullness that comes to me at each
  moment
through your promise of resurrected life.
You entice me with the wonders of this life,
and yet you draw me on with hope for the wonders of the
  future.

For all the gifts of the present,
as well as for the gifts to come,
I stand before you with gratitude.
May I have the courage to be open to the newness of life
that comes through dying.

Notice how the passing events of your life are always in a state of flux, always passing away and moving into the future. Are you able to live fully in your present moment and at the same time to face your future with a sense of hope and expectation? What sense of joy does your trustful anticipation of the future bring to your life?

Those who believe fully in the words of Christ are freed from the fear of death. Their hearts are open to the gift of resurrected life.

Jesus said to her, "I am the resurrection and the life. Whoever believes in me will live, even though he dies; and whoever lives and believes in me will never die. Do you believe this?"

"Yes, Lord!" she answered. "I do believe that you are the Messiah, the Son of God, who was to come into the world" (John 11:25-27).

"Do you believe this?" That's the challenge of Christ to you. Our belief in the promise of the resurrected life should go deeper than our heads. It needs to reach our hearts. When our hearts are convinced of the promise, then our whole being is attuned to it. We develop an intuition of its truth, and something of the promise reveals itself in a veiled way in the midst of our daily lives. And it is this intuition that deepens the meaning of our everyday lives and gives us hope.

The adventure of consciousness has its beginning on earth, and it reaches its fullness through the gift of the resurrection. Who can fathom God's love which is so generous with its gift of life? One can only begin by being awake to where one is in the present moment. Then the present moment reveals its own beauty, but it also speaks of what is yet to come. When the mind is silent, watchful, and trusting, then it understands the revelation of eternal life which God makes through his word. For such a mind, there is no longer any fear, only hope.

Consciousness is our gift when we are born into this world from the wombs of our mothers. The fullness of consciousness is our gift when we are born into the resurrected life from the womb of this world. The gift of consciousness is one that is given out of God's love. God's love for us is everlasting. So is the gift.

Thank you God, for who you are,
and for whom you have made me to be.
Thank you for your love and sharing
which never come to an end.
Thank you for the friendships with my sisters and brothers
which last into eternity.
Thank you for the total freedom
which is a gift of the resurrected life.
And so, my God, what more can I say to you?
Let me simply be silent before you,
and perhaps my silence will communicate what is in my
heart far better than my words.

In the silence, may I experience your love,
oneness with you, and with all your creation.
Let it be, my God!

Still your mind and reflect silently on Jesus' words, "I am the resurrection and the life. Whoever believes in me will live, even though he dies; and whoever lives and believes in me will never die." Be still, be grateful, and let these words rest in your heart.

Epilogue

"What does it feel like to experience life to the full?" the young woman asked the teacher. "What kind of an experience is it?"

"How can I describe it to you with words?" the teacher answered. "Just open your eyes and ears. Stay awake. And nothing will ever again be the same."

Jesus said, "I have told you this so that my joy may be in you and that your joy may be complete."

—John 15:11

When we discover what is really inside of us, we will never again be the same.

A young boy was playing in his grandparents' attic when he came across a stack of old letters buried in a drawer. As he looked at the letters, one in particular drew his attention. He observed the letter more closely and noticed that the plane on the air mail stamp had been printed upside down. When the boy showed his grandfather the letter, the elderly gentleman realized that the stamp was probably quite valuable. After checking with a philatelist, he discovered that the stamp was actually worth thousands of dollars. A treasure had been buried within his house, but for many years he had been unaware of its presence.

A treasure is buried within each of us, but unfortunately, some of us live as if it were not there. Our treasure is our ability to experience consciousness, an ever growing awareness of God and of everything that comes from God, an awareness that gives birth to love. The ultimate meaning of our lives is to be found in this awareness, for in the conscious union with God and with God's creation, we discover the wholeness which leads to our joy. This is God's will for us, that we should choose to grow in consciousness and experience our lives to the full.

Growing into greater consciousness is an experiential journey that touches every aspect of our lives. Living more deeply in the present moment, we become more aware of ourselves, of God, and of the people and things around us. Letting go of our self-centeredness, we become more alive to what lies beyond our ego's narrow vision of life. De-emphasizing our egos and our illusions about life, we become more awake to what is real. If we believe that all of this is worthwhile, we will continue our journey into consciousness with faith, persistence, hope, and joy. Letting nothing hold us back, we will give up everything in order to receive the gift that God most wants to give us—a share in his own consciousness. This is the treasure that God means for us to discover that we might share it with him and with one another in a communion of love.

> The Kingdom of heaven is like this. A man happens to find a treasure hidden in a field. He covers it up again, and is so happy that he goes and sells everything he has, and then goes back and buys that field (Matthew 13:44).

Your treasure is your consciousness, your gift from God that enables you to experience oneness with him and with the entire reality that flows from his hands. This gift is hidden within you. May you sell all so that you can fully possess this gift. May your gift of consciousness grow into the full life that God desires each one of us to enjoy.

Jesus, you have called us to follow you
and you have spoken to us that we might experience
    your joy.
You shared your way of conscious love with all of us, your
    sisters and brothers,
and then you died and rose to resurrected life.
You have pointed out the path to consciousness,
and you have asked us to make it our own.
This is the path that I choose to take,
but I can't do it without your strength,
or without the help of my sisters and brothers who share
    the path with me.

May I make the right choices,
that my journey might evolve according to your plan
    for me.
In that plan, may I find the fullness of my life with you and
    with all of creation,
both now and in the ages to come. Amen.